All the Queen's Corgis

All the Queen's Corgis

Corgis, dorgis and gundogs:
The story of Elizabeth II and her most
faithful companions

HODDER &
STOUGHTON

First published in Great Britain in 2018 by Hodder & Stoughton
An Hachette UK company

8

Copyright © Penny Junor 2018

'The Corgi Legend' by Anne Biddlecombe was first published in the
Welsh Corgi League Handbook in 1946

A CIP catalogue record for this title is available from the British Library

Hardback ISBN 9781473686748
eBook ISBN 9781473686755

Typeset in Celeste 12/19 pt by Palimpsest Book Production Limited,
Falkirk, Stirlingshire

Printed and bound in Great Britain by Clays Ltd, Elcograf S.p.A.

Hodder & Stoughton policy is to use papers that are natural,
renewable and recyclable products and made from wood grown in sustainable
forests. The logging and manufacturing processes are expected to conform to
the environmental regulations of the country of origin.

Hodder & Stoughton Ltd
Carmelite House
50 Victoria Embankment
London EC4Y 0DZ

www.hodder.co.uk

Penny Junor is a writer and broadcaster. She is the author of many best-selling biographies including of Princes William and Harry, both the Prince and the Princess of Wales and two British prime ministers. Her most recent bestseller was *The Duchess: The Untold Story*, a biography of Camilla, Duchess of Cornwall. She lives in Wiltshire with her husband and dog, Gozo.

Also by Penny Junor

The Duchess: The Untold Story
Prince Harry: Brother. Soldier. Son. Husband.
Prince William: Born to be King: An intimate portrait
The Firm: The Troubled Life of the House of Windsor
Charles: Victim or Villain?
Home Truths: Life Around My Father
John Major: From Brixton to Downing Street
Diana, Princess of Wales
Margaret Thatcher: Wife, Mother, Politician

To Gozo – a very special dog.

And to the memory of his predecessors: Dog and Divorce, Gustav, Ballou, Lupus, Raksha and Alfred.

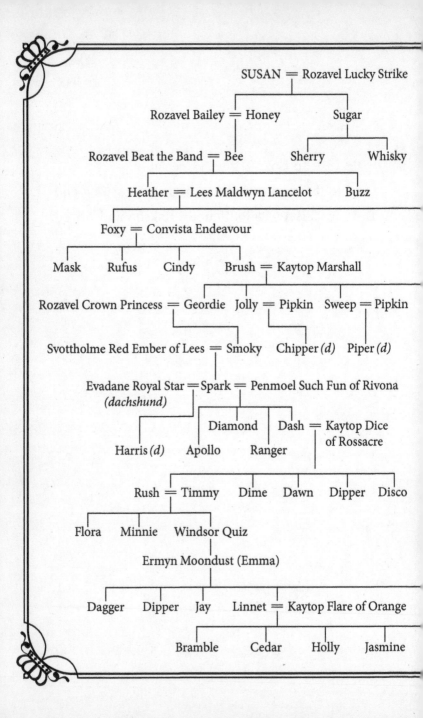

The Line of Succession
Queen Elizabeth II's corgi family tree

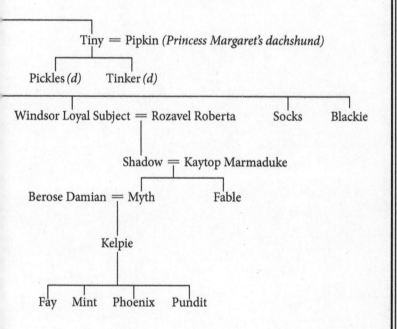

Tiny = Pipkin *(Princess Margaret's dachshund)*

Pickles *(d)*   Tinker *(d)*

Windsor Loyal Subject = Rozavel Roberta   Socks   Blackie

Shadow = Kaytop Marmaduke

Berose Damian = Myth   Fable

Kelpie

Fay   Mint   Phoenix   Pundit

> **Key**
> *(d)* = dorgi

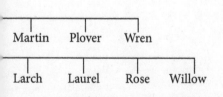

Martin   Plover   Wren

Larch   Laurel   Rose   Willow

Contents

Foreword

I have had dogs for most of my life. I grew up in a family with cocker spaniels, yellow Labradors and a very opinionated shih-tzu. As a child I thought dogs infinitely preferable to human beings. I loved them with a passion. They were my playmates and my confidantes; they shared the laughter and the tears, and my life would have been desolate without them. I entirely understand the Queen's devotion to her own dogs and the vital role they have played in her very curious life.

Our first Labrador was an impulse buy. The last cocker had met an untimely end, so we were briefly dogless. Driving home from Cornwall after our summer holiday, my father spotted a handwritten sign by the side of the road saying: 'Yellow Labrador Puppies for Sale'. He slammed on the brakes and we all jumped out, chose one and took it away with us there and then. I was no more than five, my brother ten, and the Queen was newly on the throne. I remember vividly the two of us holding this warm, wriggly, delicious creature – with needle-sharp teeth – between us on the back seat for the long journey home, while we all suggested names for him. We called him Tio, short for Horatio, and he turned out to be an indomitable character.

He was a wanderer: he would disappear for hours, usually coming home of his own accord. Occasionally we would have to rescue him from some scrape or another. Once it was from under a Green Line bus on the A24, which he miraculously survived. Another time it was from the kitchen of an irate couple whose Sunday joint he had just pinched, having walked in through an open door and found it sitting on the work surface. But the one we talked about most was the time, back in

Cornwall once again, when we drove from a house we had rented in Daymer Bay to Rock, where we left the car and travelled as foot passengers on the ferry across the Camel Estuary to Padstow. It was mid-afternoon when we realized that Tio was missing. Panic. We raced around the little town asking everyone we met if they had seen a yellow Labrador. No one had seen him. Finally, we went back to the ferry port and asked there. Someone said they had seen a dog on the ferry a few hours earlier, but it had jumped overboard a few hundred yards short of Rock.

With our hearts in our mouths and childish tears flowing, we took the next ferry, but there was no sign of Tio in Rock, either. When we reached the car, there were sandy paw prints all over the windows – he had clearly been there and tried to get in. But he had long gone.

It was getting late, and there was nothing more to be done, so we drove silently and miserably back to the house. And there, to everyone's amazement, was Tio. How he found his way there I shall never know: he had never stayed in that house before, and he had never walked from the house to Rock. It was over two miles away.

I married a man, as the Queen did, who didn't share my passion for dogs. Put off by the experience of playing emergency midwife to Tio's descendant the first time he met my family, his proposal a month or so later came with one big caveat: 'Marry me,' he said, 'but the day you get a dog you get a divorce.'

For 14 years we had cats but he knew what I hankered for so, on our anniversary, he presented me with a cardboard box. Inside were two red setter puppies: one named Dog and the other named Divorce. He couldn't resist the joke. I was pregnant with our third child, we were about to move house and red setters are crazy at the best of times; to have two together was insanity. I sent them away to doggy boarding school and picked them up two weeks – and a fat cheque – later. 'Everything I've taught them is on this tape,' said the trainer, handing over a cassette. They hadn't been home for longer than half an hour before they had chewed it into a pile of plastic splinters.

The real divorce was pending. So was the new baby. I dreamt one night that I had given birth to a litter of red setters. There was only one solution. One of the dogs had to go. So I found a good home for the boy;

six months later, the girl was stolen from our garden. My heartbreak was absolute. Gritting his teeth, my lovely husband said I must get myself another. What breed would be difficult to steal? I settled on a Great Dane, a most beautiful boy, who was run over two years later by a Triumph Stag while chasing a deer. Of all the makes of car on the road . . . But it didn't seem so funny at the time. After a few more Great Danes I settled on German shepherds as my favourite breed. I am now on my third, and a total devotee. He is funny, friendly and fearless and – I wish I could say differently – after three years, and countless hours of training, he is still a work in progress.

I have just one dog. The Queen has had up to ten at times. My admiration for her, as a dog handler alone, knows no bounds. But even the best-trained dogs can go off-piste every now and again: cock a leg over the visiting vicar or disappear into the distance, deaf to all commands. It is all part and parcel of having a dog; everyone who has ever owned a dog will have horror stories to tell. Even our sovereign has had disasters and heartbreak alongside the friendship and the fun – her mother, too.

Many years ago, at the Castle of Mey, the Queen Mother, whose sense of humour and attitude to her dogs was very like her daughter's, was ushering her lunch guests into the drawing room for coffee, when she stopped in the doorway and gazed at a large pile of poo on the carpet. 'Where did that come from?' she asked; then continued, slightly challengingly, 'It wasn't one of my dogs.' As everyone wondered what answer they could possibly give, her private secretary, Martin Gilliat, leapt in. Gilliat had been in Colditz during the war, and not much fazed him. 'Well, if it wasn't one of your dogs, ma'am,' he said, 'it can't have been one of the guests, and it certainly wasn't you, so it must have been me.'

Exploring the Queen's love of dogs during the course of her life has been fascinating and I have met some beautiful dogs and some wonderful people along the way. But most of all I have discovered an aspect of the Queen that, despite more than thirty-five years of royal writing, I have never seen before: the truly private Queen. The public Queen spends her working life in gloves and hats, gowns, crowns and tiaras; she officiates at state ceremonies and mixes with the great and the good, the world over. Off duty, she puts on casual, comfortable clothes and immerses herself in the countryside that she loves, with her dogs and horses. This is when she truly comes alive, when she is at her happiest. Dogs and horses are her passion and it is with them, and the people who share that passion, that she truly relaxes. Horses are a rich man's game but dogs are not. They are a great leveller, they attract people from all walks of life and, over the years, the Queen has had strong and genuine friendships with many of her fellow dog enthusiasts. Amongst them, she is respected not so much because she is our sovereign, but because she is a remarkably skilled handler, and a thoroughly knowledgeable breeder.

Introduction

The Corgi Legend by Anne Biddlecombe

Would you know where corgis came from?
How they came to live by mortals?
Hearken to the ancient legend,
Hearken to the story-teller.

On the mountains of the Welsh-land
In its green and pleasant valleys,

Lived the peasant folk of old times,
Lived our fathers and grandfathers;
And they toiled and laboured greatly
With their cattle and their ploughing,
That their women might have plenty.
And their children journeyed daily
With the kine upon the mountain,
Seeing that they did not wander,
Did not come to any mischief,
While their fathers ploughed the valley
And their mothers made the cheeses.

'Til one day they found two puppies,
Found them playing in a hollow,
Playing like a pair of fox-cubs.
Burnished gold their coat and colour,
Shining like a piece of satin –
Short and straight and thick their fore-legs,
And their heads like a fox's.
But their eyes were kind and gentle;
Long of body these dwarf-dogs
And without a tail behind them.

Now the children stayed all day there,
And they learned to love the dwarf-dogs,
Shared their bread and water with them,
Took them home with them even.
Made a cosy basket for them,
Made them welcome in the kitchen,
Made them welcome in the homestead.

When the men came home at sunset,
Saw them lying in the basket,
Heard the tale the children told them,
How they found them on the mountain,
Found them playing in the hollow –
They were filled with joy and wonder
Said it was a fairy present,
Was a present from the wee folk,
For their fathers told a legend
How the fairies kept some dwarf-dogs.
Called them corgis – Fairy heelers:
Made them work the fairy cattle,
Made them pull the fairy coaches,
Made them steeds for fairy riders,
Made them fairy children's playmates;

Kept them hidden in the mountains,
Kept them hidden in the mountain's shadow,
Lest the eye of mortal see one.

Now the corgis grew and prospered,
And the fairies' life was in them,
In the lightness of their movement,
In the quickness of their turning,
In their badness and their goodness.
And they learnt to work for mortals,
Learnt to love their mortal masters,
Learnt to work their masters' cattle,
Learnt to play with mortal children.

Now in every vale and hamlet,
In the valleys and the mountains,
From the little town of Tenby,
By the Port of Milford Haven,
To St David's Head and Fishguard,
In the valley of the Cleddau,
On the mountains of Preselly,
Lives the Pembrokeshire Welsh corgi,
Lives the corgi with his master.

Should you doubt this ancient story,
Laugh and scoff and call it nonsense,
Look and see the saddle markings
Where the fairy warriors rode them
(As they ride them still at midnight,
On Midsummer's Eve at midnight,
When the mortals are all sleeping!)

When historians of the future look back over the long reign of Queen Elizabeth II, they will marvel, not that she had so many dogs – throughout the centuries, monarchs, including her parents and grandparents, have surrounded themselves with dogs – but at her loyalty to a single breed. Since the age of seven, Elizabeth has not been without the companionship of a Pembroke Welsh corgi. These noisy, joyous little fox-faced dogs with upright ears and stumpy tails – not unlike mini German shepherds with their legs cut off – have been by her side, bringing a smile to her face for over eight decades.

In April 2018, she lost Willow, the last of her own corgis, to cancer (but she still has one that she took in for a friend after his death). Willow was almost 15, which is not a bad age for a corgi. The decision to have her put to sleep will nevertheless have been agonising for the Queen, albeit the kindest. She was said to have been hit 'extremely hard' by the dog's death. As a Palace source was quoted saying, 'She has mourned every one of her corgis over the years, but she has been more upset about Willow's death than any of them . . . It is probably because Willow was the last link to her parents and a pastime that goes back to her own childhood. It really does feel like the end of an era.'

Some 18 months earlier, Willow's sister, Holly, also had to be put down after an illness. Gradually, and intentionally, the Queen has been whittling down the number of dogs she has. At one time she had more than ten, but she has been typically realistic and practical in her outlook. Young dogs take a lot of looking after and you don't need to be in your nineties to be tripped up by excitable corgis underfoot. She was also concerned about what would happen to her dogs when she is no longer around. Her children all have dogs of their own and, with the possible exception of the Princess Royal, there are no great lovers of corgis amongst them.

The corgi she took in is called Whisper. He belonged

to Bill and Nancy Fenwick and was one of Willow's siblings – so it was like taking in family. Bill had been head gamekeeper at Windsor for many years before his retirement, and Nancy had looked after the Queen's dogs and helped with their breeding and whelping for 50 years. The Queen was exceptionally fond of them both; after Nancy's death in 2015, she visited Bill regularly and helped walk his dogs. When he died in 2017 at the age of 93, she offered to take in Whisper.

In addition, she still has two dorgis, Vulcan and Candy. These are a cross between a corgi and a dachshund, a combination that she has kept going alongside the corgis for several decades.

Over the years, the Queen's little dogs have travelled with her by car, boat, helicopter, plane and train; they have sat with her for photographs and portraits; they have announced her arrival in any roomful of people; and they have put countless guests, including the entire New Zealand rugby team, at their ease. Three of the corgis even walked with her to James Bond's waiting helicopter in the spoof opening of the 2012 London Olympics – one of them doing a spectacular barrel roll on the carpet. Corgis have become synonymous with the Queen and are just as recognisable. They may have been the bane of many a footman tasked with walking them or herding them up aircraft steps, but I suspect that they are the one thing that has made the Queen's curious and largely unenviable, long life bearable.

She is essentially a very shy woman, yet her whole adult life has involved being the centre of attention and meeting, greeting and initiating conversation with strangers. She has used the dogs not just to put others at their ease, but to ease her own discomfort. Her family refers to it as 'the dog mechanism'. If there is an awkward lull, she will turn her attention to one of the dogs to fill the silence, or bend down to give them titbits from her plate at the table. If the situation becomes too difficult she will sometimes literally walk away from it and take the dogs out. Prince Andrew is said to have taken three weeks to fight his way past the dogs to tell his mother that his marriage to Sarah Ferguson was in trouble.

She has described them as 'family' – and some would say she might have been closer to her own children if they had had big brown eyes, four feet and furry ears. They are an integral part of her life, and she has loved each and every one with a passion that I suspect only true dog-lovers can fully understand. Dogs are the best friends a human can ever have. They don't have moods, they don't bear grudges, they don't answer back, they don't give away secrets and they are invariably overjoyed to see their owner – especially if one is prepared to tickle their tummy. They demand nothing more than kindness, sustenance and a good walk now and then. They don't complain, they don't judge, they simply love and adore, unconditionally, and they are perhaps the only souls in the Queen's life, apart from her horses, who see her for the joyous, fun-loving human being she really is.

To us, she is Her Majesty Queen Elizabeth II, one of the most revered figures of our age, and we cannot help but treat her as anything else. Her friends, her family – even her own children – bow or curtsey to her when they see her for the first time each day. But her dogs? She will be the person they are most excited to see, the most important person in their entire universe no less, but not because she's a queen. She could be living in a cardboard box on the streets – as many dog-lovers are – and she would still be the most important person in their universe. They dote on her because she loves them, she feeds them and she is their pack leader.

As one former courtier says, 'Dogs are no respecter of position. To them she is just their mistress and she likes that.'

But when that same courtier was bitten on the ankle having accidentally trodden, one sultry summer's afternoon, on one of the corgis that ran in front of him as he walked into the Queen's study, he got no sympathy. 'Well, what do you expect?' said the Queen tetchily – obviously as bothered by the heat as her dogs. 'You've just trodden on his toe. What have you come to see me about?'

CHAPTER 1

In The Genes

It all began in 1933 when Princess Elizabeth was a small child. She and her little sister, Margaret Rose, fell in love with a neighbour's young corgi. Their father was then Duke of York, the second son of King George V and Queen Mary, and they lived in a grand, five-storey Georgian town house at 145 Piccadilly. It overlooked Hyde Park, and had 25 bedrooms, a garden and a full complement of staff. Sadly, the house is no longer there – it was bombed and destroyed during the Second World War and redeveloped in 1975 as the InterContinental London Park Lane hotel. It was a very prestigious part of London, as it still is, and their neighbours were the city's wealthiest: businessmen, landowners and aristocrats. Amongst them was Henry Thynne, Viscount Weymouth (who would become the 6th Marquess of Bath), and his young family. They had a son, Alexander, of Margaret's age, and the two sisters used to be taken to visit him.

It was there that they discovered the corgi. They already had a collection of dogs in the family; from the early days of his marriage, Princess Elizabeth's father had a yellow Labrador called Mimsy and then her offspring, Stiffy and Scrummy – a boy and a girl – while her mother had one called Rex. They were joined by a mop-headed creature called Choo-Choo, a Tibetan lion dog otherwise known as a shih-tzu, that the Duke jokingly referred to as 'the animated dish-cloth' or 'the hairy monster'. 'We called him Choo-Choo,' he explained, 'because when he first came to us as a puppy he made noises exactly like a train!' He had been a gift to the Yorks on their tour of the Empire in 1927. This pack was later swelled by the arrival of a black cocker spaniel called Ben, and Judy, a golden retriever.

But the Weymouths' corgi was so much more fun to play with than their own dogs! It raced about the garden with the children, joined in their games and had a remarkable repertoire of tricks that made them all laugh. They loved this little dog so much that they pleaded with their father to let them have one of their own. And their father, like so many fathers, could refuse his beloved daughters nothing. He discovered that his friend Henry had bought his puppy from a breeder at Pirbright in Surrey, and an equerry was instructed to write to the breeder to ask whether she happened to have anything similar for sale.

And so it was that Mrs Thelma Gray came into the Queen's life. She was one of the first people to breed corgis outside Wales, after the breed was first recognised by the Kennel Club in 1925. (The Kennel Club was an organisation set up in 1873 to do several things: to provide some rules and consistency in the new and increasingly popular pastime of dog showing and field trials; to set up stud books to record the results in championship shows; to hold a register of dogs of every breed; and to safeguard the health and welfare of all dogs. Edward VII was the founding patron, when still Prince of Wales, and it has had royal patronage ever since.) Thelma bred many a champion with the Rozavel affix[1] – and become one of the most important figures in corgi history – and also the Queen's history.

She arrived at 145 Piccadilly, in 1933, with three young red and white puppies for the York family to choose from. Two of the litter were tailless, as the breed tended to be in those days, and the third had a tiny stump of a tail.

It was the Duchess of York, Princess Elizabeth's mother, who decided which of the three they would keep. 'We must have the one which has something to wag,' she said. 'Otherwise, how are we going to know whether he is pleased or not?'

The tiny stump of a tail belonged to Rozavel Golden Eagle, better known as Dookie. He was from the very top drawer of canine families. His father, Crymmych President, and mother, Golden Girl, were both champions. His half-brother, Rozavel Red Dragon, born at about the same time as Dookie, went on to become the most famous

---

1 An affix is the name that a breeder of pedigree dogs uses to identify the strain - i.e. the kennels where they were bred. It is a means of identification in the dog world. Nowadays, the term affix (and suffix) has been replaced by the phrase 'kennel name'.

corgi ever to be shown . . . while Dookie, you could argue, went on to become the most famous corgi, full stop.

The nickname came from the kennel maids. Thelma Gray was asked to keep the pup until he was house-trained, and the girls she employed were convinced that being chosen by the duke's family had turned this puppy's head. He was so pleased with himself that he was refusing to eat from the same dish as his siblings. And so they started to call him 'The Duke'. This became Dukie and eventually Dookie. By the time he was returned to Piccadilly he responded to nothing else and Thelma Gray was left with the unenviable task of explaining to the Duke of York why this should be. So Dookie it was – and for Lilibet, as she was known to the family, it was the beginning of a love affair that has lasted her entire life.

Shortly after Dookie's arrival, the family travelled to Scotland to stay with the duchess's family at Glamis Castle, taking Dookie with them, and it was on that journey that the public first caught sight of the little dog that was to become the Queen's trademark. As the nation collectively opened their morning newspapers, they were delighted by a picture of Princess Elizabeth carefully negotiating the steps of the railway bridge at Glamis station with a small puppy on the end of a lead. His little white toes matched Elizabeth's short white socks. Dookie had made his debut.

And so it began

The public could not get enough of Princess Elizabeth in those early years. They were fascinated by her: hungry for any snippet of information, any photograph. The press, infinitely more respectful than today, did nothing more intrusive than stand outside 145 Piccadilly and peer through the railings hoping for a glimpse of her, but they speculated constantly about her daily routine, and any outfit she wore would immediately sell out in the shops. The Palace had decided that she should not take part in public ceremonies but the crowds were desperately disappointed if the duke and duchess turned up without her. Writing to Queen Mary, her mother said: 'It almost frightens me that the people should love her so much. I suppose that it is a good thing and hope she will be worthy of it, poor little darling!'

Elizabeth's grandfather, George V, was just as infatuated as the public – she was one of the few people in the country who was not afraid of him. Harsh with his own children, and impatient with his other grandchildren, he played with Elizabeth for hours, and was so tickled by her inability to pronounce her own name that he decided the whole family should call her 'Lilibet'. He allowed her to pull his beard and call him 'Big Ears'.

One visitor to Sandringham recalled the 21-month-old sitting on a small chair beside him and entertaining the whole party: 'The King gave her biscuits to eat and to feed his little dog with, the King chortling with little jokes with her – she just struggling with a few words, "Grandpa" and "Granny", and to everyone's amusement has just achieved addressing the very grand-looking Countess of Airlie [the Queen's lady-in-waiting] as "Airlie".'

When she was older she called him 'Grandpa England', which was reported with much amusement by the newspapers. He liked her to sit by him at family meals and, after lunch on Sundays at Sandringham, he would take her out with him to visit his best horses; it was he who instilled in her that other life-long passion. And when they were not looking at real horses together, they were playing make-believe: the Archbishop of Canterbury once found the king pretending to be a horse 'shuffling on hands and knees along the floor, while the little Princess led him by the beard'. And it was the king who gave her her first pony, a Shetland named Peggy, for her fourth birthday.

George V loved his horses but he was also a great

dog-lover, like his father and mother, and grandmother before him; and so it was, and has been, down the generations. It was in the genes; although Queen Mary was the exception. There is, however, a story of Queen Mary, while staying at Badminton with her niece, the Duchess of Beaufort, during the Second World War, occasionally softening sufficiently to pamper one of her hosts' dogs. She would administer a dog biscuit at the end of dinner. One night, she delegated the duty to a visiting bishop, but he, being rather deaf, misconstrued her instructions and ate the offering himself – to the delight of the family.

There was little chance the canine bug might pass Elizabeth by. Her best friend when she was only a year old was her mother's favourite yellow Labrador, Rex. The story goes that she would mouth the words 'Bow-wow' to him.

The king had owned a series of different breeds as pets – in his latter years he had a Sealyham called Jack, named after his father's favourite dog. That Jack had been an Irish terrier. Jack the younger died in 1928, when Elizabeth was two, so she would scarcely have remembered him, but he also had a Cairn terrier called

Bob. Bob (the last of many Bobs) was once left behind when the king went to Balmoral and was so inconsolable that he was never left again. He went everywhere with the king, and if the king went riding, Bob went too, running at the horse's heels.

George V was passionate about shooting – he was one of the six best shots in Britain – and the majority of his dogs were gundogs that lived in the kennels at Sandringham (built by his father Edward VII), or billeted with gamekeepers on the estate. They were a mixture of Labradors and Clumber spaniels, a heavily-built dog that Edward VII had introduced at Sandringham. The king delighted in taking his favourite granddaughter with him to visit the kennels no less frequently than the horses.

Dookie turned out to be a bad-tempered little dog by all accounts. He terrorised the household, biting visitors and courtiers alike, but the family loved him nonetheless, particularly Elizabeth and her mother. Her father was won over too, and wanted puppies from him. 'He really is the greatest personality of a dog that I have ever known,' he would say. 'So intelligent – and so marvellously patient with the children.' But he would anxiously enquire of visitors whether he had snapped at them. 'He is the black sheep of our family,' he laughingly explained to a photographer whose ankles the dog had rushed at, 'and like most black sheep, he is probably the favourite, having earned the position very unjustly.'

When Dookie was about two years old, the duke went back to Thelma Gray looking for a bitch. Rozavel Jane was the chosen bride but although the family loved her, Dookie and she were destined to be nothing more than just good friends.

The dogs were communal. When guests asked which dog belonged to whom, Elizabeth would firmly say, 'They all belong to all of us.' And, 'They are just OUR dogs,' her sister would say with equal emphasis. And they undoubtedly were part of that magic formula that made the Queen's formative years so very happy.

The family spent their weeks in London and weekends in the country: initially at White Lodge in Richmond Park and then, when Elizabeth was six, they took over Royal Lodge in Windsor Great Park, which was completely refurbished before they moved in. There were 90 acres of parkland to run around in and ride over, and, of course, the dogs came too, barking furiously and shooting off into the undergrowth in search of rabbits.

Elizabeth loved the outdoors, no matter what the weather, and declared that when she grew up she wished to marry a farmer so she could have lots of 'cows, horses and dogs'. Her parents would have liked nothing more; they had no intellectual or cultural aspirations for their daughters and kept their education to a minimum. The duchess thought education only worthwhile for women who would have to earn their own livings, while all George V demanded was that his grandchildren should learn to write legibly.

Royal Lodge had been a gift from the king in 1931 by way of consolation to his second son for giving up hunting and selling his six horses: the king had felt that it was important for the royal family to make sacrifices during the Great Depression – and to be *seen* to make sacrifices. He cut the Civil List, the money that came to the family from the state, and they all tightened their belts – if not quite as drastically as the 1.5 million people who lost their jobs, some of whom took part in hunger marches. But then everything is comparative: the duchess declared they would eat less food and drink 'weaker cocktails'.

CHAPTER 2

Every Picture Tells A Tale

For her sixth birthday, the people of Wales had given Elizabeth 'Y Bwthyn Bach', literally 'the small house', as a present, which was installed in the rose garden of Royal Lodge. It was a perfectly constructed, scaled-down version of a timbered and thatched Welsh cottage, fully furnished and impossible for anyone over 4 feet tall to stand up in. It had six rooms, running hot and cold water and a wireless set. It was a favourite haunt for the two sisters, who played there with the dogs. It was also the backdrop for some famous photographs taken in 1936 by Studio Lisa, the professional name of Jimmy and Lisa Sheridan, which appeared in a best-selling picture book by Michael Chance, published by John Murray, called *The Princesses and their Dogs.*

Sheridan was a surname randomly plucked from the telephone directory by their daughter, Dinah, who became a famous actress. Their real surname was Mec, pronounced 'mess' – the Sheridans were refugees: Dinah's father was Russian, her mother German, and they had fled from the Russian Revolution. Dinah feared that if she used her real name on stage, reviewers would say, 'An apt name! Dinah Mec's performance was a mess.' So she chose to be Sheridan and, at the same time, her parents changed their name too. Their photographic business flourished: on the strength of their commission from the Duchess of York, they went on to become photographers 'By Appointment' to both the Queen and the Queen Mother.

Today, Buckingham Palace takes a very firm line about the dogs. They are part of the Queen's private life and are therefore private and not discussed. In 1936, however, things were rather different. Those of a cynical nature might conclude that back then, the family's love of dogs was deftly used to woo the public. The Duke and Duchess of York invited the Sheridans into their various homes specifically to take photographs of them and the princesses with the family dogs in a private, domestic setting. There is no denying they are charming photographs and enough to touch even the most hardened heart. The family sat on the lawn, they sat on garden benches and walls, they hugged the dogs, the children cradled the dogs in their arms like babies; they were smiling, the dogs were smiling and all was well in the world.

Since Victorian times people had looked upon the British royal family as the model family – wholesome, virtuous and dutiful – and an important part of their role was to set an example. In the straitened years between the two world wars, the Yorks represented this ideal – and these photographs with the dogs reinforced it.

Their happy, cosy domesticity was in stark contrast to the lavish playboy lifestyle of the duke's older brother, David, the Prince of Wales. But David had the charisma that his brother lacked, and he travelled the world on it; he was charming, friendly and sincere, and a hugely popular figure. Elizabeth adored her uncle; he often came to visit them at 145 Piccadilly for games of Snap and Happy Families, and his country house, Fort Belvedere, was close to Royal Lodge. They saw a lot of one another. According to her governess, Marion Crawford (known as Crawfie), he was 'devoted to Lilibet', who was his favourite of the two princesses. He brought her presents and books, including some of A.A. Milne's. 'Changing Guard at Buckingham Palace' was her favourite poem and they recited it together endlessly. He was the perfect companion for a child as in many ways he was a child himself, with no interest in the dreary rituals of adulthood. Their other common interest was their dogs.

His dogs had the run of whatever house he happened to be in and he seldom went anywhere without at least one of them, whether it was to inspect the Guards, open buildings or bridges, lay wreaths or attend dinners. He grew up in a house full of dogs, but the first of his own was a Welsh terrier, bred by a quarryman in Blaenau Ffestiniog, which was a gift. He then had a cocker spaniel, a Sealyham that mysteriously disappeared from the courtyard of St James's Palace, never to be seen again, a whippet and a couple of German shepherds – judiciously renamed 'Alsatians' during the First World War. In later life he settled on Cairn terriers. His favourite, Cora, used to sleep on his bed, and when she grew so rheumatic she could no longer jump, he had some wooden steps specially made to help her up.

In January 1936, Grandpa England died in his bed at Sandringham. Elizabeth, aged nine, was old enough to be upset. She and Margaret had seen him just hours before he died, when he was in a coma. Later, she went with her parents to see him lying in state at Westminster Abbey, and after his funeral, Crawfie took her to Paddington station to see his body pass through on its journey for burial. The concourse was full of weeping people and as the gun carriage bearing his coffin came into view, her lip quivered but she was distracted by a fainting sailor. 'She did not like all this, but she meant to go through with it, making no fuss,' remarked Crawfie later. 'It was plain to everyone that there was a sudden shadow over the house.' But, even as a child, Elizabeth was stoic and unemotional: there was just one occasion in all her years with the family when Elizabeth solicited a cuddle from her governess, and that was after the death of her other grandfather in 1944.

It was not the first time that the innate empathy and hugability of a four-legged friend has provided comfort to someone not given – and perhaps even not encouraged – to express their feelings to others.

With George V gone, Elizabeth's beloved Uncle David became king. The public cheered him wildly. As the Home Secretary, Sir John Simon, put it: 'He was the man born to be King . . . the most widely known and universally popular personality in the world.' Yet he ruled as Edward VIII for less than a year. In November, he told his brother that he was determined to marry his American girlfriend, the twice-divorced Mrs Wallis Simpson, even if it meant giving up the throne.

Three and a half weeks later, on 11 December 1936, he abdicated, leaving the country in shock and the monarchy in peril. Bertie, his shy, stammering younger brother, Elizabeth's father, was declared sovereign. As heir presumptive he had no choice, and made it his first task as king 'to make amends for what has happened' and to restore confidence in the monarchy. He took the name King George VI to provide continuity with his father, the duchess became Queen Elizabeth and Princess Elizabeth, who had been expected to do nothing more in life than make a good marriage, became heir apparent.

Just days before the abdication, the Sheridans' charming picture book was published in time for the Christmas market and sold in great numbers all over the world. It was aimed at children, at the suggestion of the duchess, with the dedication: 'To All Children Who Love Dogs', although I fear that only the most precocious would have managed the text. But, of course, they would have enjoyed the pictures and their parents would have had to read them the words out loud – saccharine though they were – thus cementing, in both young and old alike, the conviction that the new king and his wife and children were a family of dog-lovers. What further validation could any human being need?

This is how it begins . . .

'It is no mere conventional courtesy but the plain truth that urges me to say that Princess Elizabeth and Princess Margaret Rose, together with their parents the Duke and Duchess of York, are not only deeply attached to their dogs, but – which is far more important in a dog's eyes – possess an unusual gift for understanding their animals . . .

'Accustomed as I am to meeting every kind of dog in the company of all kinds of masters and mistresses, I doubt if I have ever encountered dogs who shared with their owners a quieter or serener companionship. In other words, our Princesses and their dogs are true friends together. Which, indeed, should be the relationship between all children and their pets . . .

'. . . the two Princesses, their parents *and* their dogs constitute one very human and happy family.'

'I am afraid there are going to be great changes in our lives,' the new queen told her daughters, with more than a hint of understatement. She never forgave her brother-in-law for his selfish dereliction of duty and always blamed him for Bertie's subsequent cancer and early demise.

The York family had to give up their happy home at 145 Piccadilly, where friends and family would visit, and move to Buckingham Palace, which is more like a village than a home. It is vast, draughty and impersonal, housing not just members of the royal family but the hundreds of people employed to keep the business of monarchy ticking over. Worse still, the relaxed and doting father who had previously had all the time in the world for his daughters suddenly had to shoulder a burden for which he was ill suited and unprepared. So Elizabeth not only lost her wonderful father to duty, she also lost the beloved uncle she used to play games with - just as surely as she lost her dream of marrying a farmer.

CHAPTER 3

The Marriage Market

The move did nothing to improve Dookie's temperament. In addition to the long list of palace employees who were nipped, he bit the politician Lord Lothian, who bled profusely. And at Royal Lodge in Windsor, where the family had always gone at weekends, he had taken to attacking the dining-room chairs. He would lie low in a corner of the room while the table was being laid for a meal and, as the chairs were placed at the table, he would spring forward, lock his teeth around a chair leg and

41

growl fiercely, doing his utmost to stop it being put in place. There was scarcely a dining chair that didn't bear teeth-marks.

Jane, his intended mate, was unmoved by the chairs but she did share Dookie's enthusiasm for chasing rabbits, which were not in short supply at Windsor. The young princesses were constantly on the alert, waiting to grab a collar or shout at the rabbits to scoot. The dogs were also interested in the aviary, which housed sky-blue budgerigars. The birds had been another of George V's hobbies – he had become the first patron of the Budgerigar Society in 1930, and Elizabeth had been given a pair that she and Margaret looked after themselves, which had multiplied.

Their parents were very keen the girls should look after their own pets. They fed and walked the dogs and used to put two water bowls down for them side by side in the corridors, the hall and in each of the rooms at Royal Lodge – although it was servants who replenished the bowls with a watering can. 'Having two bowls always saves argument,' explained our future queen. 'When one dog takes a drink, it makes another think of doing the same thing – even if he isn't thirsty at all. So we put two bowls to prevent them pushing and scrambling.'

Since Dookie refused to perform his marital duty, Jane was sent off to Thelma Gray to meet a good-looking boy who was willing and able. Her chosen mate was Tafferteffy, whose breeding was impeccable but who sported a long tail, which made him useless in the show ring. Tail-docking (its amputation by one means or another) was common practice in those days,

Thelma Gray

and there were no penalties for it in the ring, but judges preferred dogs born with a naturally bobbed tail. In the intervening years, docking has been banned (under the Animal Welfare Act 2006) but there are exemptions in England and Wales for certain types of working dogs.

Despite his own tail, Tafferteffy had sired some splendid puppies that were tailless. After three tense weeks, during which Thelma kept Jane under lock and key for fear of losing her, she sent her home and pregnant to the Palace and, on Christmas Eve 1938, she had her puppies. They were all given Christmassy names, and the two that Elizabeth and Margaret kept were named Crackers and Carol.

As everyone who has owned a dog knows, the downside to letting a furry, four-legged friend into your life is that there is a racing certainty it will die and break your heart. Soon after the beginning of the Second World War, the family unexpectedly lost Dookie, long before his time. Then Carol, Jane's daughter, started having fits and she too went to the great kennel in the sky. Fortunately they still had Jane and Crackers, as well as all the other breeds. In that respect, the family were luckier than some. At the outbreak of war thousands of people in Britain had their dogs and cats and other pets put down for fear they would be killed, and others were destroyed later because of the shortage of food, or because their owners could no longer afford to feed them. Elizabeth and Margaret suffered no such deprivation – they kept their dogs, and those dogs were an important source of company and comfort during the long periods when family life was disrupted.

The two girls were secretly sent to Windsor Castle two days after Germany invaded the Low Countries. It was 'at least for the rest of the week', said Queen Elizabeth. They stayed there for the rest of the war, only seeing their parents at weekends, not so much because it was safer in the country but because it was well defended. They were kept amused by Jane and Crackers and a company of Grenadier Guards, but the castle was cold, gloomy and otherwise dull during those war years: heavy blackout curtains hung from every window, fires were only allowed in the sitting rooms and there was no other form of heating; the rooms were lit by dim bulbs to comply with lighting regulations, and all the art work, chandeliers and tapestries had been removed in case of bombing. They could not even have a bath that was more than three inches deep. In the absence of their parents, having a dog to snuggle up to, who was always full of beans, always ready to play, must have been a great comfort.

Without Dookie, Jane was top dog and bossy with it, and despite being in middle age, still very active and excitable, as the breed tends to be. But in 1944 tragedy struck: she darted across the road and was run over by one of the estate workers in Windsor Park. Elizabeth immediately wrote to the man reassuring him that she was sure it was not his fault. She knew Jane had a habit of getting excited and dashing in front of cars.

Thelma Gray, Jane's breeder, had also had a much-loved dog, a chow, killed on the road; and by the strangest of coincidences, it was the king's car that ran it over. It had happened years before, in Kensington, when Thelma was just nine years old. She was Thelma

Evans then, and the king was still the Duke of York. After the accident, he had immediately written to her parents to say how distressed he was about it and asking whether he might be allowed to replace the dog. Her parents had written back saying that because the little girl's grief had been so intense, it was probably wiser for her not to have another.

Thelma knew her parents had had a letter from the duke and, once she had recovered sufficiently, she took matters into her own hands. Without telling her parents, she wrote to him in her best nine-year-old hand-writing telling him that she would be very happy to accept his offer of a new dog. His diplomatically worded reply said that while he would have been very happy to give her a dog, he felt that both of them should accede to the wishes of her parents. There the matter rested.

Thelma ensured that when she grew up, she would never be without a good supply of dogs again. She became a professional breeder of many different breeds, including, cleverly, white Alsatians during the war – easier to see during the black-outs (she tried to get the Kennel Club to recognise the colour but failed). But of all the breeds she bred during her long career, corgis were her favourites.

Although she became a trusted friend of the whole family, Thelma never told the king that she had been the little girl with whom he had corresponded all those years before. Her story remained untold until after the king's death, when it appeared in 1955 in a book by Macdonald Daly called *Royal Dogs*.

—

CHAPTER 4

The Start of a Dynasty

On Princess Elizabeth's eighteenth birthday on 21 April 1944, her father gave her a corgi of her very own. This was the first dog that was truly hers.

Elizabeth had reached the age at which she was entitled to succeed to the throne without the need for a regent; she had graduated from her bedroom in the nursery to a suite of her own; she was given a household of her own, including a lady-in-waiting; and her own armorial bearings and her own standard, which would fly in whatever residence she was staying in. But what was really exciting was the puppy.

The bitch's official name was Hickathrift Pippa but she was known first as Sue, and finally as Susan. She was red and white – the Queen's favourite colour – as Dookie and Jane and her offspring had been, and she came from a breeder called Mr A.E. Taylor, in Cambridgeshire. Her father was Glamorous Knight and her mother, Bowhit Bonne.

Why Elizabeth's father went to Mr Taylor rather than Thelma Gray for a puppy remains a mystery. The Hickathrift kennel was not well known in the corgi world, and there is no trace of it in the 1947 Welsh Corgi League handbook; if anything, it was known for bullmastiffs. And it was not as if Thelma didn't have any puppies: a Rozavel litter, with three dogs and two bitches, had been born at the end of January. They would have been three months old by Elizabeth's birthday – and Thelma could surely have kept the puppy until April and house-trained it, as she did Dookie. One possible explanation is that the king didn't decide upon his present until the last minute. Puppies usually go to new homes at eight weeks, and good breeders often have buyers lined up before the puppies are even born. By the time the king got in touch with Thelma, it could be that all her pups had been spoken for. Susan was born a month later, on 20 February, so would have been eight weeks and ready to go by Elizabeth's birthday.

But although Hickathrift was not of particular note, the Bowhit kennel was. When corgis first started to be exhibited at small dog shows in the mid to late-1920s, there was a famous champion called Bowhit Pepper. Thelma Gray, in a book she wrote called *The Corgi*, published in 1952, says, 'The influence exerted on the breed by Bowhit Pepper was to become almost an embarrassment, since his progeny became so numerous that the problem of finding a suitable outcross for this breeding became acute. Fate stepped in, in the shape of champion Crymmych President, an excellent dog of different bloodlines, whose strain combined extremely well with that of Pepper's descendants.

'From President came Champion Rozavel Red Dragon, a record-breaking show dog and sire who, it has been said, really made the breed into what it is today.'

Whatever the explanation, it is reasonable to guess that Thelma might have been involved in finding and selecting the puppy. She had come to know the royal family well and was liked and trusted; she was also the ultimate authority on the Welsh corgi. It was she who had co-founded the Welsh Corgi League in 1938 to promote and safeguard the breed, and it was she who persuaded the Kennel Club to recognise two kinds of corgis: Pembrokes, which the Queen has, and Cardigans, which tend to be larger, longer and darker. In the late 1920s Thelma had spotted these little dogs while driving around Wales, where they originated. She sought out prize specimens that she bought from local farmers and set up a breeding programme in Pirbright. Her first great stud dog was Rozavel Red Dragon, and it was one of his offspring that went to Viscount Weymouth and started the whole ball rolling.

After the king's death in February 1952, Thelma wrote a moving tribute to him in *Dog World*, a magazine that is no longer in print; and her relationship with the Queen went on for many years.

'It was my great privilege to be received on various occasions by their Majesties in connection with the corgis,' she wrote, 'and I feel honoured that I can look back on the delightful, friendly tea parties when it was impossible to feel ill at ease, and when the whole atmosphere was the one, so familiar to us all, which always surrounds a group of people talking about their dogs.

'I think that my favourite and most treasured memory will be of an occasion when I was present at a rather stiff official function, where the king was performing an opening ceremony.

'A long line of important personages was waiting to be presented, many of them London County Council "high-ups". I was in the background in company with a crowd of other lesser fry. The King looked across, saw me, and walked straight up, hand outstretched. While I struggled with a hasty curtsey, he turned to the principal of the college and said: "Mrs Gray and I are old friends – we transact dog business together"!'

Puzzling though the puppy's provenance might be, Susan was a huge success and when the time came for her to be found a mate, it was Thelma that the Queen turned to. She selected a stud dog for Susan from the Rozavel kennels and, for the next twenty years or more, was the Queen's go-to expert and advisor on all aspects of corgis – particularly the breeding, which fascinated her. If Thelma felt that a dog from another kennels was more appropriate for a particular bitch than one of her own, she would select the dog and make the approach to the breeder on behalf of the Queen. Those breeders whose dogs were used never spoke publicly of their royal connection. Most of them, including Thelma, would often keep a puppy from the resultant litter in lieu of a stud fee.

Every corgi that the Queen has had in her very long life can be traced back to Susan – she was what is known as a 'foundation bitch' – and Susan is a famous name in the corgi world. Not so much because she belonged to the Queen, but because her genes have been so long-lived. Willow, the corgi who died in April 2018, was the fourteenth generation of Susan's descendants. And her genes could still live on, not only in the UK but in

Australia. In 1975, Thelma, then a widow, emigrated and set up Rozavel Kennels at Coromandel in the Adelaide Hills in South Australia, where she bred beagles and chihuahuas and a few Rottweilers. At the time she left she had over a hundred dogs in her kennel: as well as Pembroke corgis, she bred and showed Cardigan corgis, German shepherds, chihuahuas, beagles and West Highland terriers. She left many of them with Daphne Slake, her manageress, who went on to provide several stud dogs for the Queen, but amongst those Thelma took with her were a couple of Pembrokes: Windsor Loyal Subject, who was bred by the Queen, and his son, Rozavel Roderick. Thelma died in Coromandel in November 1984, so there is no knowing for certain if the line lives on, but it is more than likely.

Thelma and the Queen kept in touch during her years Down Under. They wrote letters and spoke on the telephone, and possibly even met during one of the Queen's many visits to Australia. After her death, her son, Jeremy, who was her only survivor, sent the correspondence to Nancy Fenwick, who gave it to the Queen. The letters are now, sadly, locked up in the Round Tower of Windsor Castle in the Royal Archives and not for public view.

One day they will make illuminating reading. As Michael Joseph Gross wryly pointed out in his excellent article about the Queen's corgis in the American *Vanity Fair* in 2015, the Palace has released numerous love letters between the Queen and Prince Philip, but the Royal Archives did not even acknowledge his request to see any correspondence pertaining to Thelma Gray and the corgis.

Meanwhile, every February, the Adelaide Hills Kennel Club, of which Thelma was a founder member, holds the Thelma Gray Memorial Show in her memory. Thanks to a generous donation from the Queen, they have a perpetual trophy in memory of the late Thelma Gray, to present to the Best of Breed Welsh Corgi (Pembroke).

CHAPTER 5

Three Of Us in the Marriage

The Queen has always referred to the corgis as 'the girls' and 'the boys', and tended wherever possible to keep at least one of the girls from a litter, thereby keeping the line intact. Susan was probably her favourite corgi of them all – in no small part, I suspect, because she had been a gift from her father, with whom she had such a special relationship, and therefore after his death the dog remained a tangible link to the man she had so adored. Susan also dates from a very special time in the Queen's life, when she was very much in love, so the dog was imbued with a lot of memories.

Elizabeth had first met Prince Philip when she was 13 and by 1944 was head over heels in love with him. They were engaged in July 1947 and married in November of the same year, when she was just 21. After the ceremony in Westminster Abbey there was a party at Buckingham Palace; in the evening, the couple left for their honeymoon in an open landau. It had started to rain but, to the delight of the crowds that lined the route to Victoria station, they forwent the comfort of a closed car and allowed the cheering well-wishers to get a good look at them. What the crowds could never have seen was what the bride had snuggled beside her. When asked about the wedding day 70 years on, Lady Pamela Hicks, Lord Mountbatten's daughter, who was one of the bridesmaids, said, 'Normal wedding chaos. The tiara broke and the bouquet was lost for a while, but the Queen was delighted to discover that her favourite corgi, Susan, had been hidden under a rug in her carriage, so that she could join them for their honeymoon at Broadlands [Lord Mountbatten's country estate].' The

Duke of Edinburgh has been vying with the dogs for his wife's attention ever since.

They had hoped for some privacy at Broadlands, near Romsey in Hampshire, but the public, whipped into such a frenzy of excitement about the couple, lay in wait – and Susan was spotted getting off the train at Winchester. After a week under siege, the threesome fled to Scotland to Birkhall, the house near Balmoral where Elizabeth and her family had often stayed over the summer, where privacy was guaranteed. She wrote to her mother: 'It is so lovely and peaceful just now – Susan is stretched out before the fire . . . and I am busy writing this in one of the arm chairs near the fire (you see how important the fire is!) It's heaven up here!'

Prince Charles was born a year later, in November 1948. By then, Susan had become so identified with Princess Elizabeth that the children's section of the *Daily Mirror* asked its readers to suggest ways to prevent Susan becoming jealous of the baby – an age-old problem for new parents when a real baby threatens to unseat a furry surrogate. 'Alan Moore, Robertsbridge, seems to speak from experience,' concluded the newspaper, 'when he says, "First. Show baby to Susan, stroking Susan all the time. Second. When nursing baby let Susan have a saucer of milk or tea beside you.'"

In May of the following year, Susan also became a mother for the first time – and the Windsor affix was born. The Queen chose her mate from one of Thelma's dogs, settling on Champion Rozavel Lucky Strike. His father was the famous Rozavel Red Dragon and he was Thelma's pride and joy. Advertising her stud dogs in the 1947 Welsh Corgi League handbook, she wrote: 'We are not detracting from the merits of our other sires, in devoting all our available space to illustrating Lucky Strike . . . Lucky Strike's marvellous type, quality bone, substance, showmanship and swank command attention everywhere and he is putting back into the breed many of its best characteristics which were sadly deficient as a result of the indiscriminate breeding during the war years . . . We have just turned down a four-figure offer for him, since we believe that if he were allowed to leave the country it would be a calamity for the breed.' To everyone else she was charging a very sizeable stud fee for him of 10 guineas [about £220 in today's money].

The Queen kept two of the bitches, Windsor Sugar, who was nominally Charles's dog, and Windsor Honey, whom she gave to her mother. She has never sold her puppies in all the years of breeding: those she has not kept herself she has given to breeders, well-vetted friends or to family. As a result, despite the Queen being patron of the Kennel Club, she did not register any of the corgis until 1971. It was only then, when Thelma Gray was given Windsor Loyal Subject – born to Windsor Brush in March of that year – and wanted to show him, that any of her dogs were registered.

Championship shows insist upon Kennel Club breed registration and full pedigree, and a special dispensation was made for the patron to register her dogs retrospectively. Not surprisingly, the records they keep are not complete and the dates are pretty hit and miss. Before she left England, Thelma won two challenge certificates (a certificate, awarded by the Kennel Club, with which a show judge states that the dog is worthy of becoming a show champion) with Loyal Subject – better known as Edward – and he was on his way to becoming an Australian champion when he was tragically killed in a kennel fight.

The Queen has never shown her dogs, and with this one exception, she has never allowed those dogs she has given away to be shown. Yet for someone who has wanted them purely and simply as companions, she has been quite particular about their looks and conformation, and very interested in perfecting their bloodlines. 'I am so fond of the breed,' she has said to friends, 'that I cannot bear to see bad ones.' And after once reading a book on corgis remarked, 'I seem to be committing all the faults of the novice breeder. I must try to do better!'

She has certainly studied them, and fellow connoisseurs whom she has met over the years say she has 'a natural eye' for a dog. 'I think,' said one judge of the breed, 'that it must come of being so long a good horsewoman. Once you understand the anatomy of a horse, you can usually pick a good dog.'

The Queen has generally preferred the dark red colour with not too much white. As the years have gone by and the breed has evolved from athletic working dog into companionable pet, a lot more white has been bred into their colouring, and this has not entirely met with royal approval. 'Oh, he's got a lot of white on him, hasn't he?' she once remarked to the former chairman of the Welsh Corgi League, Diana King, about one of her dogs. There was no mistaking the hint of disapproval.

After their marriage, Elizabeth and Philip made their home at Clarence House, across the Mall from Buckingham Palace. It was the first time Prince Philip, whose childhood had been chaotic, had a house of his own, and they and the dogs and their expanding family were very happy there.

In February 1952, when Elizabeth and Philip were staying in Kenya during a six-month tour of the Commonwealth, King George VI died. He had been ill for some time, but the news still came as a terrible shock. He had spent the day at Sandringham – 'a happy day of sunshine and sport' as Sir Winston Churchill later called it – shooting with a party of six guns. Later on, he went to the kennels to inspect one of his Labradors whose paw had been injured during the afternoon, and that evening he sat by the fireside with the queen and Princess Margaret. The next morning, his valet found him dead in his bed.

Prince Philip broke the news to his wife. She was the first monarch to have been out of the country on her accession since George I in 1714. In that moment, all semblance of normal life disappeared. Elizabeth became a queen at the age of twenty-seven; the mother of two young children – Charles, three and Anne, not yet two. Against their wishes, the family was obliged to leave Clarence House and live, instead, at Buckingham Palace. From that day forward everyone – friends, family and strangers alike – treated Elizabeth differently. The only ones who did not notice that she had become the most important woman in the land, and one of the most famous in the world, were her dogs. They were her link to reality and their demands were straightforward, consistent and easily met.

Susan was not much better tempered than Dookie – and nor were her offspring. In June 1954, Alfred Edge, a 23-year-old National Serviceman in the Grenadier Guards, was marching up and down on sentry duty outside Buckingham Palace, when a footman came round the corner with a couple of corgis on leads. Susan was one of them. She stopped to inspect the sentry box and growled at the guardsman's boots. At that very moment, Alfred Edge spotted his relief approaching and stood to attention with a loud military stamp, whereupon a startled Susan sank her teeth into his left ankle. To add insult to injury, he found himself the butt of extravagant stories, jokes and cartoons in the next morning's newspapers. Susan also bit the royal clock winder, Leonard Hubbard, and he too found himself suddenly famous. 'I was even offered the chance of appearing on television,' he said at the time, 'but I turned it down. It is all very embarrassing.'

Honey developed a taste for policemen but also shared her mother's interest in soldiers. She had just been around the gardens at Clarence House with a footman when PC Horlock, on guard duty, wandered up to them. Without provocation, Honey lunged forward and bit his knee. A royal car was ordered to take him to St Thomas's Hospital, where he was patched up and given a tetanus jab. But Honey was only just warming up. In August 1956, a young Irish Guards subaltern, off-duty and dressed in a stiff collar, dark blue suit, bowler hat and umbrella, was making his way across St James's Park when Honey raced up behind him, leapt up and bit a chunk out of the poor man's backside, tearing a sizeable hole in his trousers. His name was John Morrogh-Bernard, and he later described the incident: 'The dog was being exercised by Prince Charles and Princess Anne, and a nurse. I was a few yards away when the dog came whisking towards me, yapping loudly. I turned, the dog leaped, made one snap – and I headed back to barracks to change my clothes.'

The seven-year-old Charles was very apologetic. He ran after Lt Morrogh-Bernard, making anxious enquiries about his welfare, but the subaltern assured him he was fine and kept running. The damage to his rear was surely nothing compared to the damage to his dignity.

CHAPTER 6

The Power of Influence

Notwithstanding the current explosion of designer '-doodles' and '-poos' – the result of cross-breeding of almost any breed with a poodle – that have become so ubiquitous in the UK, the country's most popular pure breed is now the French bulldog. In the last ten years there has been an unprecedented increase of 2,964 per cent in the number registered with the Kennel Club. And for the first time since 1990 (when it took over from the Yorkshire terrier), it has knocked the Labrador off its perch as top dog, and pushed the cocker spaniel another rung down the ladder. Since about 70 per cent of dogs in the UK are not registered, the size of that increase could be a lot higher.

Cocker spaniels were the second most popular dog in the UK in 2017 at 23,000. No prizes for guessing who has a cocker: the Duke and Duchess of Cambridge. The lovely Lupo made his debut in 2012 as an adorable bundle of black fur, and immediately the number of searches for cocker spaniels on the Kennel Club's 'Find a Puppy' service shot up by almost 50 per cent. They refer to it as 'the Kate Middleton effect', and say it comes with a very strong health warning. 'Working cocker spaniels . . . are highly active and need constant stimulation so they will not be suitable for everyone.' The number of unwanted dogs that are handed in to rescue centres like Battersea is testament to that.

The Kennel Club puts this sudden spike in French bulldogs down to fashion and celebrity ownership. The Beckhams, Lady Gaga, Leonardo DiCaprio, Reese Witherspoon and Hugh Jackman all have one. And celebrities are not only photographed with their dogs, they post cute images on social media. And what those on our screens do, the rest of the country shall surely follow. For years our televisions have shown that adorable yellow Labrador puppy, romping through a pristine house tangled in a roll of 'soft, strong and very long' loo paper – and we have wanted one just like it.

And so it was more than eighty years ago with the Pembroke Welsh corgi. When Princess Elizabeth was seven and was photographed carefully crossing that railway bridge in Glamis with Dookie, the breed's fortunes began to look up. In those days before television, let alone social media, when celebrities were fewer and further between, she was the nation's pin-up. What she and her family did, the nation followed – and once the Yorks were known to have a corgi, a breed few people beyond rural Wales recognised at the time, they started appearing in households all over the country.

It was Queen Victoria, Elizabeth's great-great-grandmother, who started the trend for keeping dogs as pets. Kings and queens as far back as the eleventh century had dogs, as did much of the general population, but it was Queen Victoria who gave them the status in our lives they have today, and she had more of an influence on what dogs her subjects chose to keep than any other monarch before her. She had more than a hundred dogs during her life, and 28 different breeds, many of them very exotic, received as diplomatic gifts from across the globe: chow chows, Havanese, Eskimo dogs, Skye terriers, Scotties, Pomeranians, Pekingese, Maltese, pugs, collies and dachshunds, while her husband, Prince Albert, kept mostly greyhounds and beagles.

Her first dog was a Cavalier King Charles spaniel, given to her by her mother, the Duchess of Kent, when she was a child. It was called Dash and according to her biographer, Elizabeth Longford, he was 'the Queen's closest childhood companion'. At the age of 13 she wrote in her diary: 'I dressed dear, sweet little Dash in a scarlet jacket and blue trousers . . .' For her seventeenth birthday, her mother gave her a portrait of the dog, painted by Edward Landseer – just one of many portraits of Victoria's dogs that have been left to posterity. When Dash died in 1840, he was buried in the grounds of Windsor Castle with the epitaph:

'His attachment was without selfishness,

His playfulness without malice,

His fidelity without deceit,

READER, if you would live beloved and die regretted, profit by the example of

DASH.'

Before Victoria's time, Britain was not the sentimental nation of animal lovers we are today. Cats were skinned alive, and dogs were regularly used to bait bulls or to fight one another for public amusement. Cruelty was commonplace, and there was no attempt to curb it until 1822, when Victoria was just three years old. Martin's Act was a breakthrough – the very first animal welfare law ever passed – but it did nothing more than forbid 'the cruel and improper treatment of cattle'. Two years later the Society for the Prevention of Cruelty to Animals was founded – the first animal welfare charity in the world. Its biggest challenge was to get the British public to recognise that animals were sentient beings and not merely commodities to be used for food, transport or sport. The nascent Society had some early success but it was financially insecure, and there were fears it might fold.

Fortunately, the teenage Victoria and her mother came to the rescue. They honoured it with their patronage, without which the first Bill for the protection of domestic animals, in 1835, might never have been passed. The Pease's Act consolidated Martin's Act and prohibited cruelty to dogs and other domestic animals, bear-baiting and cock-fighting were forbidden, and it insisted on better standards for slaughter houses. Victoria continued to be the Chief Patron after her accession in 1837, and in 1840, she permitted the Society to use the word 'Royal'. It thus became known as the RSPCA.

She went a long way to change attitudes. She was seen to treat her dogs well and she encouraged others to do the same: and not just dogs. She actively supported the RSPCA throughout her reign; she also gave her patronage to the Lost Dogs' Home at Battersea, where she persuaded the committee to keep all dogs for two days longer than the law required.

The public followed her example in all things. And, largely thanks to her influence, today, the biggest international dog show in the world is a British institution. Charles Cruft was a goldsmith's son who started out, aged 14, as a post boy with the revolutionary new dog-food company, Spratt's. He quickly progressed to better things within the firm and by the age of 26 was in charge of the office and sales department. The job took him all over the country, visiting kennels and estates, and he became involved in various dog breed clubs and put on shows for them.

By 1896 he had had enough of organising shows for other people and, at the suggestion of the Duchess of Newcastle – a formidable presence in the male-dominated dog scene – put on one of his own. Billed as the 'First Great Terrier Show', it became an annual event; in 1891 he renamed it 'Cruft's Greatest Dog Show' and, with a lot of hype, opened it up to all breeds.

It was held at the Royal Agricultural Hall in Islington and, crucially, attracted the attention of Queen Victoria. No one knows quite how Charles Cruft achieved it, but she, the Prince of Wales – later Edward VII – and her son-in-law, King Haakon of Norway, were all persuaded to exhibit dogs – the first time royalty had ever entered a dog show. The publicity it attracted arguably sealed the success of Cruft's (the name lost its apostrophe in 1974) for ever.

Queen Victoria entered four dogs: Darnley II, a rough

collie, and three of her Pomeranians: Gino, Nino and Fluffy. Darnley and two of the Poms won prizes, while the third got a Very Highly Commended. The Prince of Wales sent along four of his rough bassets, which won every prize in their class. To add to the glamour, Tsar Alexander III of Russia; his son, Grand Duke Nicholas – soon to be Tsar Nicholas II; and Prince Constantine Oldenburg also competed one year, sending 18 champion Borzois to the show, there being no quarantine restrictions at that time.

After Edward VII's succession in January 1901 – Queen Victoria died with a Pomeranian on her bed – he and his wife, Queen Alexandra, were regulars at Cruft's. They were provided with a sumptuous and very visible royal box, furnished in the queen's favourite colour blue, but she often left it to visit the benches to get a closer look at the smaller dogs, taking a particular interest in the Pekingese and West Highland White terriers.

She doted on dogs and throughout her life had probably a larger collection than any other royal figure. She had dozens of different breeds – and a menagerie of other animals – and, like her husband, abhorred any form of cruelty. She allowed no gun to be fired near the gardens at Sandringham, condemned society ladies who wore osprey feathers and thoroughly disapproved of fox hunting. She was so opposed to the common practice of cropping dogs' ears to make them point upwards, a sentiment shared by her husband, that he protested to the secretary of the Kennel Club. The letter was viewed as a royal command and, thanks to him, it was banned in 1897 (although it is still rife in many other parts of the world).

Edward VII had a variety of exotic breeds but his last dog was a wire-haired fox terrier called Caesar, who was noted for neither his looks nor his good behaviour, but he was mischievous and intelligent and the king doted on him. He wore a tag on his collar with the legend, 'I am Caesar, the King's dog'. Caesar was his constant companion: he walked at his heels, he slept on an armchair by his bedside and he sprang up for titbits at the table.

When the king died, Caesar was inconsolable and spent days whining pitifully outside his master's bedroom door, refusing to eat. Eventually Alexandra was able to coax him to back to normality. On her instructions, on the day of his funeral, Caesar walked behind the gun carriage carrying the king's coffin. Vita Sackville-West was one of the millions who was there and recalled 'everyone cried when they saw the King's little dog following the coffin'. The little dog was the supposed narrator of an enchanting bestselling book published in 1910 called *Where's Master?* After his death four years later, he and his master were symbolically reunited when his recumbent figure was carved at the king's feet on Edward's tomb in St George's Chapel, Windsor.

An instant bestseller

Throughout her widowhood, Alexandra was a regular sight at dog shows all over the country, and also at Cruft's with her son, George V. She entered Pekingese, Japanese spaniels, basset hounds, Borzois and a Samoyed, but was particularly fond of her Borzois. She had initially been given two by the tsar – and Borzois were soon in all the most fashionable homes. George V showed his Labrador retrievers, entering them for the first time in 1916; in 1932 and 1934 he won first prize with his Clumber spaniel, Sandringham Spark.

By then Cruft's was recognised as the largest dog show in the world; in the Jubilee show in 1936, it had over 10,000 entrants and in 2018, that figure had risen to 27,000 with more than 160,000 visitors – 15,000 more than went to the Glastonbury Festival.

Charles Cruft died in 1938, and his widow took it over briefly. It was abandoned during the war years, and when it restarted in 1948, it was under the auspices of the Kennel Club, of which George VI was then patron. It still runs Crufts and field trial championships, yet despite the Queen, as a young princess, having been to a Welsh Corgi League show in 1947, at which she said she would like to show her dogs 'if only I had the time', she never has done so. And despite having taken over the role of patron of the Kennel Club within months of her father's death, she has only been to Crufts once in her reign, in 1969.

Only two snippets of conversation were recorded from the Queen's visit to Crufts. She is said to have asked an official: 'Why do dogs yawn?' Having cordially listened to his explanation that the yawn 'communicated tension from the handler to animal', she ventured her own belief that one of her corgis yawned 'when it didn't want to do what it was told'. Her other remark was equally surprising: 'I've had one of my corgis trained for working cattle.'

CHAPTER 7

The Pembroke Corgi

Herding and driving cattle is not an obvious calling for a dog that stands no more than 30 cm high, but it is what these dogs were originally bred for. They did it by running behind the animals, barking and nipping their heels – being small and agile enough to dodge an angry hoof when it lashed out. And it is that instinct to herd – to bark, to nip and to dodge – that was alive and well in so many of the Queen's dogs, and which was highly prized in their native land.

Much of what is known about the breed was handed down from old Welsh farmers, who remembered the tales their grandfathers told them. They would say that there were always corgis on the farms to do the work; the dog was indispensable to them, and without it they would have had to employ another hand to do the work of one dog.

In 900 AD when Wales was governed by a ruler known as Hywel Dda – 'king of all the Welsh' – he drew up laws to put a value on domestic animals in case of loss or theft. A cattle dog was deemed to be of the same value as 'a steer of current worth'. And since there is no evidence of any other cattle-herding dog indigenous to Wales, it is reasonable to assume this dog was none other than a corgi.

They drove cows, bullocks, mountain ponies and other stock for miles, sometimes to markets as far away as the Midlands and even London. And folklore has it that while the drovers would settle down to a well-deserved pint of ale at the end of the long trail, the dogs would take themselves home. They were also used to hunt rabbits and keep down mice and rats. The only task they were not so good for was herding sheep, for all the reasons that made them so good with other livestock: they were too sharp and excitable. And while they have been used as gundogs, they struggle to carry the weight of a cock pheasant.

Where the name came from is a matter of opinion. The most likely explanation seems to be a simple combination of the Welsh words 'cor' meaning 'dwarf' and 'gi' meaning 'dog'.

As for its origins, some say it is descended from vallhunds, Swedish cattle dogs that were brought to Wales by the Vikings in the ninth and tenth centuries. Others think it was Flemish weavers who brought the ancestors of the present-day Schipperkes and Pomeranians, Spitz-type dogs, in the twelfth century. There are also more fanciful theories, of which the poem at the start of this book is the most common.

A variation tells of a battle between two warring fairy tribes, the Tywyth Teg and the Gwyllion, which resulted in the deaths of two of the Tywyth Teg warriors. Two human children, out in the fields tending cattle, happened upon the funeral procession and were gifted the departed warriors' noble steeds to help them with their herding. The dogs, they were told, 'are trained warriors in their own right, but they are more than warriors: they are great helpers for the fairy folk'. They would be perfect for herding cows, explained the Tywyth Teg: when they nipped at their heels, the dogs' diminutive size would keep them out of the way when the cows kicked out.

And if they nip their owners, it is said that that is because fairies don't give gifts without strings attached. The way to stop it is to attach a bit of iron or steel to their collar – because fairies have a natural aversion to both metals.

Devotees of the breed are not surprised by the Queen's unswerving loyalty to Pembroke Welsh corgis. They deem the many pluses of the breed to outweigh the occasional assault on the ankle. They are bright, bold, lively, loving, courageous and intensely loyal – however much their detractors might point out that they bark

Dookie and Jane – an
arranged marriage that
never bore fruit.

A girl's best friend.

The family already had several dogs but 'Lillibet' persuaded her father to add a corgi to the collection.

Queen Elizabeth with Elizabeth and Margaret – dog lovers all.

Princess Margaret with Sealyham terriers but it was her dachshund that started the fun.

The Queen has always insisted on good manners at feeding time.

SUSAN
BORN 20th FEB 1944
DIED 26th JAN 1959
FOR ALMOST 15 YEARS
THE FAITHFUL COMPANION
OF THE QUEEN

She had always dreaded losing Susan.

Nicky Philipps' portrait for Royal Mail –
she finally got them all to sit still.

The sisters
and their
dogs on
the move.

uite a handful.

Handover on the tarmac:
Nancy Fenwick - 'Keeper
of the Queen's Dogs'.

They may not all be devoted to corgis but her children are all dog lovers.

In her element.

Dogs will always roam royal corridors and romp by the River Dee. The Prince of Wales, William, Harry and Widgeon at Balmoral.

Lively Jack Russells could be the next incumbents. Charles and Camilla with Beth and Bluebell.

What greater love?

As we will remember the Queen: joyfully surrounded
by her faithful companions.

incessantly, race around underfoot, are easily trodden on or tripped over and have a propensity, even without provocation, to draw blood from any stranger foolish enough to proffer a friendly hand – or be walking along minding his own business.

Breeders over the last 50 years or so have been trying to improve the temperament and breed out the tendency to bite but it has been in the dogs' DNA for thousands of years and while most corgis are benign these days – also lower to the ground, and less athletic – there is the odd throw-back. Before Thelma Gray forayed into deepest Wales and found two specimens to her liking from which she started to breed, the corgi had scarcely been seen beyond the Welsh hills.

For many years after the Kennel Club first recognised Welsh corgis in 1925, the Cardigans and the Pembrokes (known as the corgis with and without a tail, respectively) were lumped together as one breed under the category 'Any Other Varieties Not Classified'. Today, thanks to Thelma's lobbying, they are registered as two distinct breeds and are classified as 'Pastoral', along with breeds like collies, sheepdogs and shepherd dogs. The Cardigan is the older of the two, thought to have been in Wales since around 1200 BC. It is one of the oldest breeds in the British Isles, and is descended from the Teckel family of dogs, the same family that produced the dachshund.

Over the years, the Cardigans were probably cross-bred with collie and fox-terrier types of dogs, possibly to make them more useful. And there has no doubt been some interbreeding with the Pembrokes too, particularly before the distinction was officially recognised. Their colourings are similar to the Pembroke, which can be red, sable, fawn and tri-coloured (red, black and tan) usually with white on the legs, chest, neck, muzzle and belly, but Cardigans can additionally be brindle, brindle and white and blue merle. Pembrokes should have straight front legs, whereas the Cardigan's should be slightly bowed, and the Pembroke's head is more refined and its ears smaller in proportion to the head, while the Cardigan's ears, as well as being larger, are often rounded. To the average pet owner these are insignificant details. In most other respects the dogs are very similar, yet ever since the two were recognised as different breeds in 1934 – a year after Dookie arrived in the York household – the Pembroke corgi has far outstripped its cousin in terms of popularity. That year, 250 Pembroke corgis were registered, compared with only 59 Cardigans, which one can only assume was down to their royal connection.

During the early years of Elizabeth's reign, in the 1950s and 1960s, the Pembroke's numbers rose dramatically. In 1950, Pembrokes were up to 4,342, with Cardigans lagging behind at just 168.

Numbers peaked in 1960 at 8,933. Nowadays, they are back in the mid to low hundreds and alas, because the Queen is now in her nineties, corgis have been seen for some time by many as old people's dogs. Recently, their numbers had fallen to so few that the Kennel Club put them on their list of native breeds in danger of extinction, but, thanks to the popular Netflix series, *The Crown*, in which the young Queen Elizabeth, played by Clare Foy, is inevitably seen with corgis, the breed has had a reprieve. After the second series was aired in December 2017, the number of people searching for corgi puppies on the Kennel Club website increased by 22 per cent.

To think of corgis as a suitable breed for the elderly is to wildly misjudge them. They are not toy dogs, and although they like nothing more than to hop up onto a lap and cover it in hair – corgis have thick coats that moult all year round – they are not really lap dogs, either. As every owner will tell you, they have all the attributes of a big dog in a little dog. They are hugely athletic and despite those little legs need a lot of exercise, or they become very overweight. They can walk for miles and give any squirrel a run for its money. They are also very strong willed and need firm handling. After all, in terms of the history of the breed, they have been pets for less than a hundred years but working dogs for twelve times that, and possibly longer. It would be surprising if they did not still have a few residual traits.

CHAPTER 8

The Expanding Family

In 1955 Susan's daughter, Sugar, was sent off to Thelma's kennels to be mated with another Rozavel stud, a handsome boy called Rebellion. Thelma also managed the whelping at her kennels and in due course took the litter to Windsor to show them to the Queen.

Charles and Anne were with the Queen when she met the puppies and although she had every intention of keeping just one, when she saw them, she could not make up her mind. 'Don't tell your father,' she instructed the children. 'Don't tell your father we've got two puppies. Two new puppies!' She named them Whisky and Sherry, and gave them as Christmas presents to Prince Charles and Princess Anne.

The two people entrusted with looking after all the royal puppies was the head gamekeeper at Windsor, George Hallett, and his wife, who had worked for George VI. They were very knowledgeable about dogs, as all gamekeepers are, and undertook a lot of the training, particularly the house-training. From time to time they were charged with taking care of all the dogs if the Queen was out of the country and the Queen Mother was unable to have them.

The Halletts retired in 1964 and this was when Bill and Nancy Fenwick came into the Queen's life. Bill was appointed head gamekeeper. 'I do hope the new game-keeper's wife likes dogs,' the Queen was heard to remark, and as luck had it, she did. The Fenwicks had been living at Camp Hill, an estate in North Yorkshire with their two sons, where Bill had stepped into his father's shoes as head gamekeeper. He had been in the post for 16 years when he saw the job at Windsor advertised in the *Shooting Times* and came south. They moved into a grace-and-favour bungalow in the Home Park, a stone's throw from the castle. It had a garden that was securely fenced to keep in adventurous corgis. Bill was 40, just a couple of years older than the Queen; Nancy was just a few years younger, and they developed a remarkable relationship based on a mutual passion for dogs and shooting, which lasted until Bill's death. Nancy was 84 when she died, and such was the Queen's devotion to the woman jokingly referred to as 'The Keeper of the Queen's Dogs' that she attended her funeral in person, something she rarely does for anyone other than family.

Bill and Nancy's bungalow became a home from home for the corgis and the dorgis. They had dogs of their own: as a gamekeeper, Bill had gundogs, which he trained himself, but there were plenty of indoor pets as well. Nancy was a dog-lover through and through and, like her husband, was very knowledgeable and competent with them. But you would never have known it to look at her. A tall, slender woman, she was always immaculately turned out, with not a hair out of place, even when wrestling with five or six obstreperous dogs on the ends of leads. Her real love was Tibetan spaniels, but she took to the corgis with enthusiasm and had a blue merle Cardigan corgi herself at one time, as well as corgis and dorgis given to her by the Queen. What with her own and the Queen's, the house was overrun with dogs and there was no chance of any visitor reaching the front door without a discordant chorus of barking.

Nancy took the dogs whenever the Queen was unable to have them with her – she acted in loco parentis – and although she did not drive, she would travel in a royal car with them to meet the Queen, either to collect or dispatch them. She was a familiar if inconspicuous sight at airports, where there was many a handover on the tarmac.

She became indispensable to the Queen, and she was one of the very few people whose calls would be put through to her, no matter the time or day. She became heavily involved in the corgi breeding programme and came to know Thelma and the girls at the Rozavel kennels well.

Nancy was also a valuable link between the Queen and the corgi community – all members of the Welsh Corgi League, of which the Queen is a great supporter. Her face will light up whenever people with corgis are

waiting amongst the crowds to see her on public engage-
ments, as they do all over the world, and on three
occasions the Queen has invited the East Anglian section
of the League to bring their dogs and have a walk in
the grounds and gardens at Sandringham. On each occasion she has joined them, quite informally, made a fuss
of their dogs and chatted freely, as one corgi lover to
another. The last time they were there, in 2013, there
were no fewer than 60 members, and she spoke to every
one of them.

The League produces an annual handbook, which lists
all the breeders; also a calendar, with a picture of
members' dogs illustrating each month. Members are
invited to submit photographs. One year, Nancy
submitted a spoof photograph of an extremely long
corgi, its head sticking out of one end of a long tube,
its rear out of the other. It was in fact two different
dogs, and although she insisted the name of the
photographer must be given as 'Anonymous', no one
doubted whose dogs they were.

Breeders came to know Nancy well, and when the
Queen was looking for a stud dog, where it had once
been Thelma who made the approach, it became Nancy.

She and the Queen worked very closely together and had an extraordinary friendship. More often than not, the mating – and the whelping – would take place in Nancy's kitchen, to which the Queen was a frequent visitor. To the amusement of some of the breeders, the custom for the bitch to go to the dog did not apply, but most of them were more than happy to take their stud to Nancy's bungalow in Windsor, where they would invariably meet the Queen. She always wanted to see the dogs and assess their looks as well as their temperaments before choosing the one she wanted to use. Stud fees were rarely, if ever, offered. There was usually the offer of a puppy in lieu, but they didn't always get the one they asked for.

Neither Sherry nor Whisky had litters, but the Queen Mother bred from Sugar's sister, Honey. Honey was mated with Rozavel Bailey in 1956 and produced Bee, who in the fullness of time was mated with another of Thelma Gray's dogs, Rozavel Beat the Band. The Queen Mother did not keep any of that litter but the Queen took two of the puppies, Heather and Buzz.

Heather became a mother in 1965 to Foxy and Tiny but their sire, for the first time, was not a Rozavel dog, although he would almost certainly have been of Thelma's choosing. The lucky boy was Lees Maldwyn Lancelot, from a kennels in Sussex, owned by Pat Curties, with a string of champions in his ancestry including some Rozavels.

Both Foxy and Tiny had litters: from Foxy, the Queen kept Mask, Rufus, Cindy and Brush, and from Tiny, who had an unplanned liaison with Princess Margaret's dachshund Pipkin, she kept Pickles and Tinker. Brush was mated with a highly acclaimed stud called Kaytop Marshall that belonged to Leila Moore, who became a regular source of sires. She bred for 'a clean-cut outline, level topline, true and strong hindquarters', and Marshall was her best ever dog. He was 'a charismatic showman of the richest possible red colour and amazing presence', who sired four UK champions. Had Windsor Loyal Subject lived longer, that score would have almost certainly been five.

Before Loyal Subject emigrated, he was mated with Rozavel Roberta, who produced a litter from which the Queen took a pup that she named Shadow. Shadow then produced Myth and Fable, and in 1984, Myth produced Kelpie, who was a great favourite and the longest lived of all her corgis. She died at the age of 17 in 2002 – the year the Queen also lost sister and mother.

But we are getting ahead of ourselves. Loyal Subject's siblings were Jolly, Sweep, Socks, Geordie and Blackie – of which the latter two went to the Queen Mother. Between them, mother and daughter were building up a very large, and potentially murderous, pack of dogs; when the Queen's flight landed at Aberdeen for the family sojourn at Balmoral in 1981, she was said to have 13 corgis with her. And as any dog-owner knows, the more dogs, the more disagreements, even amongst relatives.

Thelma used Geordie (who you will remember was Loyal Subject's brother, owned by the Queen Mother) to sire a litter from Rozavel Crown Princess, and although neither of them kept any of his puppies, the Queen had one of his granddaughters, Spark, who was born in 1978. In the summer of 1984, two months after Myth had whelped, Spark also produced four puppies that did join the royal pack. The Queen kept Diamond, while Ranger and Dash went to the Queen Mother – who by this time was 84 – and Apollo went to Princess Anne, the Princess Royal, the only one of the Queen's four children who has ever shown any interest in corgis. Princess Anne's son, Peter Philips, is the only grandchild to have liked the breed. Shadow then produced Myth and Fable, and Myth had Kelpie, who went on to have Fay, Mint, Phoenix and Pundit.

And this is the abridged version!

Dash was mated with Kaytop Dice of Rossacre, owned by Ally Broughton, and produced Rush, also Dime, Dawn, Dipper and Disco. By 1992 the Queen was looking for a suitable mate for Rush. Nancy spotted a potential one at the Windsor Dog Show, held every year at the end of June in the Home Park. Breeders come from far and wide and Mary Davies, current chair of the Welsh Corgi League, and her husband Jeff, had come from Kent with Ermyn Quest For Fame, better known as Timmy. Mary had first met Nancy at the show a few years earlier, introduced by Pat Curties. (It was two of Mary's dogs, incidentally, that played the Queen's corgis in Peter Morgan's 2013 play, *The Audience*, starring Helen Mirren, about the Queen and her prime ministers.) The Davies also have horses, and had bought a racehorse called

Landmark at the Newmarket sales that they subsequently discovered the Queen had bred. When the Queen arrived at Nancy's bungalow to take a look at Timmy, 'dressed as we all do when we walk our dogs – in wellies, a mac and headscarf', Jeff mentioned they had had a win with Landmark; apparently, the Queen was not just interested, she immediately rattled off the horse's bloodline off the top of her head.

She made a fuss of Timmy and looked at him, complimented them on his 'nice face' and then remarked, 'He's very quiet, isn't he? And steady.' Quiet and steady was clearly what she was looking for, because Timmy was chosen from seven other dogs that were brought to Nancy's for inspection. 'He was a calm dog,' says Mary but, as she points out, it is not surprising the Queen's dogs can be a bit hyper. 'They don't have the same lifestyle as ours. Ours know where home is and they know who everybody is, the same people handle them. But the Queen's dogs go off to Windsor, then they're off to Sandringham and then Balmoral, and in each place they are meeting lots of different people and being exercised by different people, and it's exciting, it gets their blood up. The Queen's favourite footmen like the dogs but not everyone who deals with them does. Corgi puppies, actually any puppies, will grab hold of the bottom of your trousers. We laugh but if you don't like dogs you might not find it so funny, and the puppy will remember if someone has kicked him away.'

Timmy and Rush had four puppies, a boy and three girls. The Queen kept two girls, Flora and Minnie, and gave one, Windsor Quiz, to Mary. Quiz went on to have a litter four years later from which the Queen took Ermyn Moondust, which she called Emma. Emma then produced Dagger, Dipper, Jay, Linnet, Martin, Plover and Wren.

Linnet was the mother of the last litter of corgis that the Queen ever bred. Bramble, Cedar, Holly, Jasmine, Larch, Laurel, Rose and Willow, sired by Kaytop Flare of Orange, were born in Nancy's kitchen in 2003.

Is it hardly surprising then, that Prince Philip, who dislikes the breed anyway, should have been heard to complain irritably: 'Bloody dogs! Why do you have to have so many?'

CHAPTER 9

By Accident and Design

Princess Margaret never truly caught the corgi bug. Although she loved Dookie and Jane when she was a child, as an adult she was more interested in working dogs. Sealyhams had become very fashionable, especially those bred by the MP Sir Jocelyn Lucas, under the Ilmer affix. His were bred as sporting dogs – used as beaters to flush out pheasants and rabbits, and to go to ground after foxes and badgers. He also bred the eponymous Lucas terrier, said to be 'death to rats'. They appealed to Margaret and she took delivery of a boy called Ilmer Johnny Boy when he was six months old. She took him almost immediately up to Balmoral where, unhappily, within days she took to her bed with measles. She and Johnny were separated and in her absence he forged a strong bond with the Queen Mother.

Margaret never had the number of dogs her sister and mother had, but she did get another Sealyham, and when she was married to Lord Snowdon she also had a Cavalier King Charles spaniel, and a black Labrador. But the dog she most famously owned was a smooth-coated miniature dachshund called Pipkin.

Vertically challenged though he may have been, Pipkin was not put off by taller women: one fine day in the late 1960s, he and the Queen's corgi, Tiny, had an illicit moment together behind the shrubbery. Actually, history does not relate where or quite how it happened (perhaps the clue is in the name Tiny), but we can be sure it was not in Nancy Fenwick's kitchen, and approximately 62 days later, a new crossbreed was born.

Proving themselves years ahead of the trend for portmanteau names, the Queen and Princess Margaret called their creation 'dorgis'. It was the beginning of a new royal era.

The first litter was always believed to have been a mistake – not to mention feat of canine engineering – but Elizabeth and Margaret were so pleased with the outcome, a boy named Pickles, that they deliberately mated Pipkin again. First with Jolly, and then Sweep, producing, respectively, Chipper and Piper. Both boys. When royal photographer Norman Parkinson once asked the Queen how the corgis and dachshunds were able to mate, given their rather different heights, she replied: 'It's very simple. We have a little brick.'

The Kennel Club has never recognised crossbreeds. It will record them on their Activity register, of dogs involved in canine sports like agility, obedience and flyball, but all varieties, whether Heinz 57s or designer, are lumped together under 'Crossbreeds'. When asked at the time about the Queen's new creation, the Kennel Club replied, 'The dachshund was evolved to chase badgers down holes, and the corgis to round up cattle. If anyone loses a herd of cattle down a badger hole, then these are just the dogs to get them out.'

The Kennel Club's stance is simple. There are no

guarantees about crossbreeds and no consistency about how they will look or how they will behave. In their experience, it takes between 25 and 40 generations of a breed to be able to predict type and temperament with any certainty. To create a new breed, you would keep crossing the crosses, choosing only to breed from the individuals that displayed the looks and character-istics you were trying to achieve – 'So you are looking at a project that is going to take decades.' The designer crossbreeds are mostly first generation, so inevitably they display varying characteristics from the two breeds in their make-up.

The name 'dachshund' means 'badger dog', so as she had previously had Sealyhams, which went to ground after badgers, it is perhaps not surprising Princess Margaret should have moved on to dachshunds. They were bred to chase the animals out of their setts so they could be shot. A miniature version was subsequently developed so they could be used to root out smaller animals such as foxes and rabbits, although they also readily killed rats. Queen Victoria's favourite dachshund, Däckel, a gift in 1845 from her German cousin, Prince Albert's elder brother, Ernst II, Duke of Saxe-Coburg and Gotha, was an ace rat catcher. He once pounced on an enormous rat in the presence of the queen, who remarked, 'the rat made an awful noise, though he was killed outright pretty quickly'.

They are fearless little creatures that were used as sporting dogs for centuries; that much is beyond dispute. Where they originated is less certain, but according to Zena Thorn-Andrews, who is a leading expert on the breed, long-bodied and low-to-ground types of dogs were definitely known in central Europe in the Middle Ages and possibly even earlier, and there is evidence that similar types of dogs were in Britain too until the twelfth century. They were used to hunt beaver and badgers. There are several references to them by name in a rare book called *Cynographia Curiosa seu Canis Descriptio 1685*, by Christiano Francisco Paullini. The author even refers to the breeding of miniatures: 'Give powdered nitrum, as much as remains on a moistened finger-tip, three or four times every morning to a bitch in whelp from a week before whelping and to the pups until six months old. This through its "coldness" will prevent development and keep them quite small.' Although others will say the miniature was developed by selective breeding, this book does prove beyond any doubt that the breed was known by its present name in Germany in 1685.

Victoria had her first dachshund, Tiko, in 1837 – Albert sketched a portrait of his head – and her affection for them spread to the general population. From 1860 they began to be imported by a Mr Schuller, who sold hundreds, and in 1881 dachshund owners formed a club that is still going strong today, claiming to be one of the first clubs for any breed in the world.

Victoria had 14 generations of dachshunds, which ensured their popularity endured, and apart from a blip during the First and Second World Wars because of the German connection, they have been one of the most popular small breeds in the UK ever since. They come in three different coats: smooth-haired, long-haired and wire-haired, and can be standard size or miniature. They are all equally noisy, brave, stubborn, funny and loyal, with a penchant for sleeping under the duvet and the intelligence to make it happen.

The only things that have been consistent about the Queen's dorgis is that they have all been smaller than their mothers and they have all had tails; but some have been fluffy, some short-haired, some ears have gone up, some ears have hung down. They have also all barked as loudly and ferociously as their mothers.

The Queen was not intent on creating a new breed. She regarded the dorgis as a bit of fun between her and her sister, and they were such friendly little dogs they kept on doing it. The puppies that they did not keep went to friends, estate workers and anyone who came recommended that would be sure to give them a good home. Bill Meldrum, who was in charge of the gundogs at Sandringham, found homes for many of them amongst locals. He and his wife, Annie, have even had two themselves over the years: Emma and Pixie. He remembers the Queen once inviting those people to a dorgi party at Sandringham, to which everyone was told to bring 'wellies and dorgis', for a walk followed by tea. 'I'm not coming to a dorgi party!' this very tall, masculine Scotsman told the Queen, when they were 40 yards from the house. 'Yes, you are!' came the firm reply. Then she said: 'Meldrum, would you hold these dogs for me for a moment? I've forgotten my camera.' He took the two dorgis in his arms, and she ran off back towards the house, then called out 'Meldrum!' again. As he turned she took a photograph. 'I've got you!' she said, triumphantly.

Bill Meldrum came 'for a few years' and stayed 41

When Pipkin was no longer around to do the honours, they had to find other breeders, and again it was Nancy Fenwick who had her ear to the ground. She made contact with Anne Hazelby, who bred miniature long-haired dachshunds in Marlow under the Evadane affix.

It was just before Christmas when Nancy telephoned to ask whether they might use her red-coated stud dog, Evadane Royal Star, known as Rory. Anne had no idea that it was at the Queen's request and was initially uncertain, not really being a great believer in cross-breeding; she wanted to speak to her vet first to make sure that he approved. He thought it would do no harm, and so she agreed, but in common with so many corgi breeders, was surprised by the request to take the dog to the bitch. But as soon as she discovered who owned the bitch, she was happy to take him.

The thought of meeting the Queen terrified her. What would she say to her? She was half hoping she might not come, but the Queen did indeed come to inspect the dog, although she was running late. 'And he had to bark at her, of course,' says Anne. But despite her fears, the meeting with the Queen could not have been easier. 'She was a joy to talk to,' she recalls. They were simply two doggy people having a conversation about their beloved animals.

Rory stayed with Nancy over the entire Christmas period, while Anne and her husband went to visit their daughter in Devon, and in due course his puppies were born. The Queen named them after Scottish islands. She kept Harris for herself, Margaret Rhodes, her cousin, took Rum and Nancy Fenwick was given Stroma. Anne was offered the remaining pup, but since she already had a number of dogs and would not be able to show or breed from this one, she declined.

And so, as always, the puppy was given away to a friend. They were always given on the understanding that they were not to be bred from. Nancy also made clear that the Queen liked to be given updates on how the puppies were doing, and her interest was obviously genuine because if people wrote, the Queen would always write back.

A few years later, in the 1990s, Nancy again approached Anne Hazelby and asked whether she might use Rory's son, Reggie, another red-coated, long-haired miniature. The Queen always used miniatures, she said, because she thought the standards too big. Anne duly took him to Windsor but this particular blind date did not work out. And so Anne recommended a friend of hers, the late Joanne Wilson, a fellow breeder under the Coalacre affix, who had had one of Reggie's pups, and they used him.

There was just one occasion when the Queen and her sister did breed to the second generation. At the end of November in 1990, Anne Hazelby had a call from Nancy asking whether she had a dachshund bitch she might let Rum, Princess Margaret's dorgi, mate with. Anne did have a suitable red bitch called Evadane Golden Pride, better known as Heidi, but she was hesitant. She got in touch with her vet once again. What were the implications of her miniature having these larger, cross-bred puppies? The vet was satisfied no harm would come from it, reassuring her that the mother dictated the size of the puppies, and so Anne took her bitch across to Windsor. The mating was successful, Heidi went home for her pregnancy and a litter of three boys and a girl were safely born at Anne's kennels on 21 January. She delivered them to Nancy when they were seven weeks old.

The Queen was delighted with the result but it would

appear that she never repeated it. The cross-breeding was something she and her sister had done together, but Princess Margaret became unwell several years later, and died in 2002; soon afterwards the Queen Mother died too. It was not long after that that the Queen decided it was time to wind down the breeding programme. She had taken on her mother's corgis, which had upset the equilibrium of the existing pack of eight: four corgis – Emma, Linnet, Willow and Holly; and four dorgis – Cider, Berry, Vulcan and Candy. To those she added her mother's dogs, Minnie, Rush and Monty. So she had more than enough on her hands.

Besides, Nancy may have been four years younger than the Queen, but by the early 2000s, she was in her seventies and thinking about retirement. It would have been hard work looking after such a large number of dogs, particularly boisterous young ones – and a few quarrelsome characters – in addition to the whelping, rearing and house-training of puppies.

The Queen was also concerned that young dogs might outlive her, leaving her family with the dilemma of what to do with them: a stance the Kennel Club wholeheartedly applauds.

Since Nancy's death, care of the dogs has fallen sometimes to footmen but mostly to the Queen's trusted dressmaker, assistant and right-hand woman, Angela Kelly; and to her equally trusted page of many years standing, Paul Whybrew, who was seen walking with the Queen and the dogs in the James Bond spoof. Both are fond of the dogs, have unfettered access to the Queen and are said to be very close to her.

CHAPTER 10

Kennel in the Sky

Susan lived to the age of 15, which is not bad for a corgi. But in January 1959, she became mysteriously unwell during the Queen's Christmas break at Sandringham and was taken to the local vet, Harold Swann. He was in practice in King's Lynn from 1933 until his retirement in 1973, and looked after the Queen's dogs when problems arose on his patch for most of that time. But she also had a vet in Windsor and another in Scotland, so he did not know the dog's full history.

Speaking ten years later to colleagues at the opening of an extension to a veterinary centre and hospital, he described the day Susan was brought into his surgery:

'. . . the greatest reward we can have in our work, I think, is the appreciation and kindness shown by an owner when things go right, whether it is a child with a pet hamster, or newlyweds with a pet given them as a wedding present, or a widow on her own with a pet dog as her only friend in the world – the appreciation shown, as I say, when things go right is something we always treasure.

'We realise that dogs and cats mean an awful lot to an owner whatever their walk in life, and we often find that the illness of a pet is a great leveller. To illustrate this, I thought perhaps you would like to see a letter here which we actually received from the Queen. Some time ago one of the footmen from Sandringham brought in one of the Queen's dogs. He hadn't the slightest idea what was wrong with it or what the symptoms were. I wrote on a scruffy piece of paper some questions which I wanted him to find answers to.

'When he came the next day, he said to me, "The Queen has written the answers to your questions on this piece of paper." I thought you would like to see what she said. It so happened that this particular dog was a very special pet of hers and we suspected that it had a tumour of the liver. The message was passed to her and I suggested that it should go to the College at Cambridge for an operation, and I asked what would be her wish if the condition was hopeless – should it be put to sleep under the anaesthetic? And the reply came back that this was what she wished us to do.

'It so happened that our diagnosis was right and the dog was destroyed and the Queen wrote us a very nice letter which again I thought you would be interested in reading. Needless to say, it is gratitude of this sort that keeps us all going and makes us so very interested in our job.'

The questions he had written on a scruffy pad of headed notepaper, dated 21 January, and the Queen's answers, scribbled in pencil on the same pad, were as follows:

1. How long getting bigger?
   No idea – she's always been fat! Possibly noticeable a week ago.

2. Thirst? *Yes, particularly after meals.*

3. Ever had puppies? *2 litters 1948, 1949*

4. Any discharge when in season?
   Isn't regular any more as will be 15 in April but think it was in October or November.

And the note was signed 'ER'.

Susan, sadly, died on 26 January. Three days later, the letter to which Mr Swann referred was delivered to the surgery. This one was written in ink on Sandringham-headed notepaper inside a hand-addressed envelope. Harold died in 1994, but his daughter Carole Harrisson has the correspondence.

Dear Mr Swann,

I would like to thank you for all you did for my dear old Susan when she became ill, and for the immense amount of trouble you took in getting her sent to Cambridge and for all the care she had while she was there.

Perhaps you could express my thanks to your colleagues?

I had always dreaded losing her, as I had had her since she was six weeks old but I am so thankful that her suffering was so mercifully short – she was very happily beating for us out shooting on the Friday before!

With renewed thanks

Your sincerely

Elizabeth R

Susan was buried in the pet cemetery at Sandringham that Queen Victoria had created in 1887 for her collie, Noble. Victoria grieved for all her dogs, as her journals repeatedly testify, and started the custom of erecting elaborate headstones for them. For some she even had statues made. Edward VII was equally sentimental about his animals, as was his wife. Queen Alexandra was so distraught when Togo, her favourite Pekingese, died in 1914 that she laid him on a cushion in her bedroom and refused to let him be taken away. After two days the smell was intolerable but she was adamant.

According to Queen Alexandra's friend Zoia Poklewski-Koziell's mother, Baroness de Stoeckl: 'That day at tea there were some egg sandwiches. The Queen smelt them and then said with tears in her eyes, "Just like my sweet little Togo." Zoia started laughing and she became almost hysterical. The Queen saw the joke and started herself and they laughed and laughed. Zoia, seeing the good mood, said, "For goodness sake, Ma'am, have him taken away or I shall never be able to look at an egg." "All right," said the Queen. So Zoia flew out of the room, met a page and gave the order. Togo was buried. The next day a new Togo arrived, a gift from Lady Arthur Paget, and all was in order once more."'

Queen Elizabeth is no doubt every bit as grief-stricken as her forebears were when a beloved pet dies, and only time will tell what she has confided to her journal over the years, but she is not a sentimentalist and she is not given to showing emotion. She is a country woman, she understands that nature is 'red in tooth and claw' and she is generally very matter of fact in all things. But once, when one of her corgis died, and Lady Pamela Hicks wrote her a note of condolence, she had a very moving six-page, very personal letter back from the Queen, explaining just how deeply she felt about the dog. Something she could possibly never have done about a human being.

Victoria's dogs were buried in the garden of the residence in which they died, something Queen Elizabeth has continued; there are cemeteries at Windsor and Balmoral, too. At Sandringham it is hidden away in a quiet corner of the garden, near a boundary wall inset with memorial stones, amongst daffodils, and there are touching tributes to dozens of dogs there, both pets and gundogs.

After Susan's death, the Queen wrote to her estate manager with instructions for her burial and drew a sketch of the gravestone she would like, and the inscription she wanted carved into the stone:

Susan

died 26th Jan 1959

for 15 years the faithful companion of the Queen.

She followed this with another letter, after she had found Susan's date of birth: 'So could you have that inserted between her name and her death on the stone, please?' Two weeks later she wrote again: 'My only comment is that for accuracy's sake we ought to put for almost 15 years. The rest's quite alright.' She underlined the word 'almost' and signed the note 'ER'.

When Susan's daughter Sugar died in July 1965, she was buried alongside her mother, with her dates and the same legend: 'For over 16 years the faithful companion of the Queen.' Heather, who died in January 1977 and went into the same plot, was credited with being not only the faithful companion for 15 years, but also 'Great Granddaughter of Susan'.

By the 1990s the Queen had become more descriptive. Sandringham Fern, a roan cocker spaniel, was 'Tireless Worker and Mischievous Character'. Sandringham Brae (of whom more later) was: 'A Gentleman Amongst Dogs.'

What she chose to write about Willow, the last of her corgis, who is buried at Windsor Castle, is not known.

'A gentleman amongst dogs'. The Queen had her greatest success as a handler with Brae.

CHAPTER 11

It's a Dog's Life

The Queen's dogs do not eat out of shiny sterling silver dishes. Pampered they may be, but the Queen is nothing if not practical; their bowls are a motley collection of metal and porcelain. They do, however, eat exceedingly well, and their diets are tailored to their individual needs. In the country they get a lot of rabbit shot on the estates; otherwise it is a variety of fresh, cooked meat, vegetables and rice, prepared specially for them in the royal kitchens, topped with a little biscuit, homeopathic and herbal remedies when required and a special gravy that, legend has it, is the Queen's own recipe. Whenever possible, she feeds them herself and it is an afternoon ritual; but not an unruly frantic free-for-all. A footman brings the food and the bowls on a silver tray and lays out a plastic sheet to protect the carpet. The Queen then sits them in a semi-circle around her and does the rest.

Roger Mugford, the animal psychologist, who was brought in after some dramatic dog fights, watched her do it and he was impressed. As he wrote in his book, *Dr Mugford's Casebook*, 'It was 4 pm and time for the dogs' meal, when problems may have arisen between them. The Queen looked across to the semi-circle of quiet but salivating dogs congregated a few metres away and called each one in turn to take his or her food. There was never a growl or rude look between the dogs and I was amazed at the harmony which reigned indoors at this theoretically high-risk time. The Queen explained that she had always been strict in requiring good manners amongst the dogs at feeding time and each was obliged to wait his turn, the eldest to be fed first and youngest last. There is barely anyone else on the planet who could achieve that control over their dogs.'

They did it for the Queen because they were her dogs and she was their pack leader. But dogs have a habit of being deaf to commands from anyone else and feeding time in her absence was not always so calm. When she was away it would fall to a footman to feed the corgis – whichever footman happened to be on duty – and experience and love of dogs was not in the job description. It is said that one footman, who was bitten during the feeding frenzy, took his revenge by lacing the dogs' dinners with gin. The Queen was unamused when she found out, and although the man managed by the skin of his teeth to stay at the Palace, he was demoted and (to his joy) never allowed to have anything to do with the dogs again.

In addition, the dogs get titbits from the Queen's own plate at mealtimes – toast at breakfast, scones in the afternoon and chicken, fish or whatever else she is eating at lunch and supper. They cluster around the table, even when she has guests, and attend all the best parties. The only events they are excluded from are those where there is a danger they will get under someone's feet. And they are not invited to state banquets, although I am sure the Queen sometimes wishes they were. They are not only an immediate and easy topic of conversation, they are invaluable at helping visitors, who can be completely and sometimes irrationally tongue-tied on meeting the sovereign, relax.

One such person was David Nott, a saint of a surgeon from Wales, who works for ten months of the year as a consultant in three major hospitals in London, and for two months volunteers his expertise in conflict surgery in the world's most dangerous war zones. He is now in his early sixties and has been doing this for the last 25 years. He has saved countless lives in that time, many of them children's, in places like Bosnia, Gaza, Darfur, Congo, Afghanistan and Syria. The day he went to lunch with the Queen he had just come back from Aleppo, centre of the fiercest fighting in the Syrian civil war. He had been operating in a makeshift hospital as he invariably does, with basic instruments, often by torchlight through power cuts, while barrel bombs exploded and shook the earth around him. 'Saving life is a wonderful thing,' he has said. 'When you salvage a patient from the brink of death you feel euphoric.'

Two years earlier the Queen had awarded him an OBE, and at the lunch table he found himself seated on her left-hand side. It was October 2014 and he had only been back in the UK for ten days. It usually takes him three months to re-adjust. When she turned to talk to him he could not speak. 'I was thinking about the day when seven children from one family were brought into the hospital,' he told Frances Hardy in the *Daily Mail*. 'Their mother was dead and one of her sons had his buttocks blown off. He was still alive and he had white blobs on his face. These were his sister's brains. It was the most pitiful sight I'd seen in twenty years operating in war zones. I couldn't save him. All I could do was comfort him and hold his hand.

'When the Queen turned to me and said, "I hear you've just been in Aleppo," I could feel my bottom lip quivering. I couldn't say a word. There's no doubt I was suffering from post-traumatic stress. All I could do was stare long and hard at the wall.

'She realised something was terribly wrong and said she'd try to help me. Then she started talking about her dogs and asked if I'd like to see them. I said I would. I was trying not to cry, to hold it all together, and suddenly a courtier appeared with the corgis, who went under the table. Then a silver tin with a screw-top lid labelled "Dog biscuits" was brought to the table. The Queen opened it, broke a biscuit in two and gave half to me, and she said, "Why don't we feed the dogs?" We kept feeding them and stroking them for half an hour or so as she chatted and told me all about them.

'The humanity of what she did was unbelievable. She was really so kind to me. And afterwards when everyone asked what I'd done at the palace they couldn't believe what I told them. She was so warm and so wonderful I will never forget it. She wasn't the Queen any more but this lovely person with a human face. There's no doubt she helped me.'

The Queen has five residences dotted about the country and corgis and their paraphernalia are a familiar sight in all of them, but none more so perhaps than Buckingham Palace, where she does most of her entertaining and conducts most of the business of state. They are very much part of the furniture there, but they sleep inside the Queen's private apartment. There is a special corgi room where they have raised wicker baskets lined with cushions to keep draughts away, but which comfortable spot they choose to sleep on at night-time is anyone's guess. The only outsider who has seen the Queen in bed was Michael Fagan, an unemployed decorator from Clerkenwell, who famously broke into Buckingham Palace in 1982, and found his way to the Queen's bedroom. It was 7.15 a.m. and the dogs were out having their early morning walk with Paul Whybrew (then her footman), one of the most senior and trusted members of her household.

Had Fagan come any earlier, the dogs would have seen him off. Even if they had not been in her actual bedroom, they would have sensed an intruder and made such a racket that someone would surely have come running.

If Fagan had come much later, however, their barks might have been drowned out by the sound of bagpipes. Every morning at nine o'clock sharp, when the Queen is in residence, the Sovereign's Piper, resplendent in tartan, marches up and down along the terrace outside the Queen's windows for 15 minutes playing her favourite tunes on the bagpipes. It is a custom that began with Queen Victoria in 1843, who after hearing this music for the first time on a visit to the Highlands, appointed Angus Mackay as her personal piper. The sovereign has had one ever since.

The bagpipes, it has to be said, are something of an acquired taste. And while the Queen loves them, and is fascinated to know the story that is behind every tune written for them, the corgis and dorgis – with one notable exception – slink away. 'The pitch of the pipes seems to hurt most dogs' ears,' says Jim Motherwell, the former Pipe Major of the Argyll and Sutherland Highlanders who served as the Queen's piper between 1997 and 2003. 'But there was one little corgi called Linnet who, whenever she saw me get my pipes out, used to follow me around.'

The only royal residence the piper does not play in is Sandringham; otherwise, he follows the Queen to Windsor, to the Palace of Holyroodhouse where she spends a week at the end of June and to Balmoral for the summer. And it is there in the Highlands, the land of the bagpipes, that he plays the most. At the end of dinner every night he plays his way down a corridor and into the dining room, where he makes two circuits of the table and retreats.

His room at Balmoral was next to the senior footman's room, where Linnet, as a young puppy, was being babysat in the summer of 2000, the year she was born. 'So I was in and out when she was small and I would be tuning up the pipes in my room and I suppose the little dog got used to them.' The same cannot be said for Linnet's siblings, however, who headed for the heather when Jim began to play.

With its acres of forests and moorland bristling with wildlife, Balmoral is a dog's paradise. And the Queen's four-footed friends are allowed the freedom to enjoy it. The late Lady Margaret Rhodes, who was her first cousin and childhood playmate, used to walk with her for miles. She once said, 'They're often rather unruly, the dogs. They chase rabbits like mad. There are a lot of rabbits around Balmoral, certainly, and the Queen gets excited with the dogs chasing the rabbits, egging them on. Telling them to, "Keep going, keep on going!" She also takes herself off on long solitary walks with the corgis; they help take her mind off things if she is anguished or frustrated. "If you have had constraints about not talking, you need some outlet," she said. While she and her husband talk freely, she does let loose with her dogs.'

She is still walking her dogs – albeit not quite as far as or as fast as she once did. When her programme permits, it is part of her daily ritual. They are not as agile as they once were; she and they have all slowed down together. But, arguably, walking dogs most days of her life is what has kept the Queen so fit and so mobile.

The director, Michael Waldman, who has made several documentaries about the Queen, remembers a wet day at Balmoral and the dogs coming back into the castle, through the front door into the hall, and being carefully towelled dry by the footman who had given them their morning walk. Michael came away with the impression that this was not to keep wet paws and sodden coats off the antique rugs and sofas, but to ensure that the dogs didn't catch a cold. At least one of them was elderly, and their tummies do sit very close to the ground.

There is obviously far less wildlife at Buckingham Palace – although, according to Margaret Rhodes, after it was bombed during the war there were rats that the Queen Mother used to shoot. But while it may be in the centre of London, there is a surprisingly large garden behind it, as anyone who has ever attended a Jubilee concert or a summer garden party will know. There are over 40 acres, including a four-acre lake, and the dogs know every inch of it. As soon as the garden door is opened for their walk, they shoot off excitedly across the lawn, barking and running after pigeons and squirrels.

If the Queen is in London for the week, she normally goes to Windsor Castle for the weekend – it is less than an hour's drive down the M4. Nowadays, she and the dogs usually make the journey in separate cars but, as she told Roger Mugford, time was when she would pack them into an old Vauxhall estate and take them for a spin herself, wearing a headscarf to avoid being recognised. However, even now, once they are all safely in the country, be it Berkshire, Norfolk or Scotland, she will drive them about the estate, often in an ordinary Land Rover or a Range Rover. They are fewer, older and more sedate these days, but at one time there were anything up to ten dogs scrambling over the seats, bouncing from front to middle to back, and back again, barking furiously at everything they passed.

CHAPTER 12

Family Squabbles

It was the sheer number of dogs the Queen had that brought Roger Mugford to Windsor Castle in 1984. He had a telephone call from Philip Ayrton Grime, from the Hillbury veterinary practice in Windsor. Grime had a client, he said, with several dogs that had begun fighting. As he started questioning him the vet came clean: his client was Her Majesty the Queen, the dogs were corgis and several people had been bitten while trying to separate them, including the Queen Mother and Prince Edward.

The Queen had heard about Roger from Princess Anne through Riding for the Disabled, of which she is patron, and where he had done some work. He met Grime at his surgery and went over the clinical history of all the dogs. She had ten at that time – seven corgis and three dorgis – who had most commonly been to the vet because of dog fights, not ill health. Given that the males in the pack were 'entire', he thought it not surprising there had been the occasional scrap. 'These were not just mild scraps,' he was assured. 'Blood had been spilled.'

They travelled to the castle together, where they were taken up staircases, along corridors and through doors to meet the Queen in her private apartment.

Roger's wife had drilled him in royal etiquette, all of which he forgot, along with his nervousness, at meeting the sovereign. She greeted him warmly and immediately the talk was of the dogs. Thereafter she could have been any client – with a great sense of humour and a devotion to her dogs. There had been fights in the castle, in the grounds, in cars and at Buckingham Palace – dramatic gang fights and fallings out over something as simple as a dead mouse. But significantly, they had not fought when they were with either the Queen or Nancy Fenwick.

Having grown up with corgis as a child on a farm in Devon, which earned their keep by swinging fearlessly from the tails of cows too slow to come in from the fields, Roger Mugford was familiar with the breed and had personal experience of their penchant for nipping ankles. 'It's in their DNA,' he laughs. 'If it runs, make it run faster!' But fighting was not.

The dogs met them in the garden. All ten were let out of a side door and came charging towards the Queen, barking at Roger and the vet, until Myth, one of the younger ones, submitted to a game of roly-poly and a tummy rub. He observed how they interacted with one another. Piper, a dorgi, seemed to be the troublemaker. He was young and jostling for position – and as the family had joked, was 'ostentatiously macho'. He was pestering Chipper, another dorgi, the oldest male and traditional top dog. His advice was to take Piper out of the equation. So the dog was duly dispatched to Princess Anne's home at Gatcombe in Gloucestershire, where he was kept in his place by her lurcher.

But his major observation, having spent two hours at

Windsor, was that the Queen had too many dogs – which she readily accepted. She had become 'a collector'. Prince Philip, she confessed, told her the same thing. Roger had expected to find that control was the issue, that she was not especially competent at handling them, but that was not the case at all. She was a skilful, observant, capable owner, and authoritative, not over-indulgent, not spoiling. The fact that no fights had broken out on her watch indicated that she had top-dog status. But it would be a challenge for anyone, he says, to manage such a big group, particularly when she often had the Queen Mother's dogs in there, too, and Princess Margaret's.

There was another challenge, which the Queen also readily accepted. She had a very busy schedule, which involved a lot of travel, so management of the dogs inevitably fell to a number of different people, which greatly complicated things. At Windsor alone there were 30 or 40 individuals who had interactions with them, and not all of those people were dog savvy. There were two who were deputed to look after the dogs in the main – 'Tall Paul' and 'Small Paul', one of whom was particularly good with them – but they worked shifts and had holidays and days off. And these were smart working dogs that were easily bored.

'Look, ma'am,' he said candidly. 'Don't get any more, your hands are too full.'

The Queen heeded his advice, and this was why Piper went on a one-way trip to Gloucestershire, and harmony was restored amongst the pack. But to ward against similar incidents in the future, Roger left the Queen with a device called a 'Dog Stop', which he had been working on to prevent owners having to physically pull fighting dogs apart and risk being bitten. The idea for it had come about when he had seen a pair of Jack Russells successfully distracted from their fight by the dramatic clang of a dropped dustbin lid, and he realised the answer was something loud – and more portable than a dustbin lid. What he came up with was a variation on a rape alarm.

Unhappily neither the Queen, nor the alarm, were around on the terrible day in 1989 that a massive fight broke out between her dogs and the Queen Mother's corgis. The ring leader was Ranger, the Queen Mother's dog, who attacked Chipper, a dorgi, by this time an elderly dog, and 'ripped him to shreds'. Two years later there was another major fight between the two packs, when the Queen presumably did not have the alarm on her, either. She tried to intervene and was so badly bitten on the left hand, she needed three stitches, while the Queen Mother's chauffeur needed a tetanus jab.

There was another, equally distressing incident in 2003 when the Princess Royal arrived at Sandringham on Christmas Eve with her three bull terriers: Florence, Eglantyne and Dotty. The doorbell alerted the corgis to their arrival. Five of them, who had been in the upstairs sitting room with the Queen, went racing down to the front door. As it was opened, Florence pushed in and savaged Pharos. The Queen had had a knee operation so had to wait for a lift to take her down, and by the time she arrived at the scene, it was too late: the dogs were locked in mortal combat. Pharos was 13 and no match for the powerful terrier. She clamped her jaw onto his back leg and shook him like a rag doll. They managed to pull the dogs apart with the help of some footmen but the leg was badly broken in three places and the following day, to the Queen's great distress, he was put to sleep.

Anne had a run of bad luck with her bull terriers.

The year before, she had pleaded guilty to being in charge of a dog that caused injury in a public place under the Dangerous Dogs Act, and was fined £500: another bitch called Dotty had bitten a child in Windsor Great Park on Easter Monday, two days after the death of the Queen Mother. Like so many dogs, Dotty was obsessed by moving wheels, and when she spotted two little boys riding their bicycles, shouting excitedly, the combination of wheeling and squealing was irresistible. While Anne and her husband, Commodore Tim Laurence, were putting their dogs into the back of the car, Dotty made a run for it, and raced over to the children barking wildly. The children 'may have panicked', the court was told. They both fell off their bikes, one was nipped on the leg and collar bone and the other was scratched before Dotty responded to Anne's command to 'come' and trotted back to the car. Once they were safely shut inside the princess went to apologise. Both were undoubtedly traumatised, but neither of them needed stitches.

Roger Mugford was asked by Anne's barrister to give his professional assessment of Dotty's temperament and character, and he attested in court to the dog's fundamentally good nature. He described her as a 'totally placid, playful, tolerant dog', who momentarily lost her head but was eminently trainable. To the disgust of the children's relatives, the dog was given a stay of execution. Anne was ordered to have her trained, which Roger undertook, and to keep her on a lead at all times in public places.

Anne came away with a criminal record. It could have been worse. The burden of proof lies with the defendant and Roger's evidence was crucial. 'You know that if I go down,' she joked, 'you'll be spending a few years on Saint Helena!' (Saint Helena was the island in the South Atlantic to which Napoleon was exiled.) Roger was also successfully brought in to speak up for Florence, who, shortly after the Pharos incident, bit a maid who was trying to clean Anne's bedroom.

CHAPTER 13

Artists' Secret Weapon

The artist Nicky Philipps was lost in the one-way system around Holborn. She had driven around it at least four times and was in a fury when her phone rang and her agent said, 'I've just had a call from Royal Mail. I think this might be quite exciting.'

'To paint who?' she asked crossly.

'Think about it, Nicky,' came the reply, 'think about it . . .'

She was being asked to paint a portrait of the Queen

for the commemorative Diamond Jubilee first-class stamp. It was the commission of a lifetime and came to her, she thinks, as a result of the highly acclaimed painting she did for the National Portrait Gallery the year before of Prince William and Prince Harry. They are depicted standing together in their Blues and Royals lieutenants' uniforms and you can almost hear the banter. They themselves chose her to do the painting, having seen an example of her work in a catalogue, and they came to her studio in South Kensington for five 90-minute sittings. 'No one knew of me before that,' she says.

With only three one-hour sittings on offer, she asked the photographer, Ranald Mackechnie, who has worked for Royal Mail over the years, to come with her on the first sitting to take photographs that she could then work from. All they needed for the stamp was a portrait of the Queen's head, but it never occurred to her to ask Mackechnie to take head shots. 'He stood a reason-able distance away and took lovely full-length photos. When I saw them I thought, I want to do her as head of state. I really want to do a gorgeous, majestic portrait – you always think you can do it better than anyone else! And Royal Mail said I could do what I wanted –

but they would only use the head. So I went berserk. And then I thought I am going to make this much more fun. I'm going to put the dogs into it.' She asked the Queen if she could. "Yes, okay," she said. "You had better have Holly," assuming that I would only want one.

'I said, "I would really like to use all of them," knowing that at that point she had four: two corgis – Holly and Willow, and two dorgis – Vulcan and Candy.

She expressed surprise.'

Nicky started again on a larger canvas – a really huge canvas – and the result now hangs in the Throne Room at Buckingham Palace. The Queen stands straight and resplendent in the collar and robes of the Order of the Garter over a white dress and a crimson sash over her left shoulder. She is every inch the majestic head of state but, massed around her feet, are her dogs – and Holly is standing cheekily on her train. She has cleverly encapsulated the two sides of the Queen that we all know and love.

The dogs were not invited to the sittings. She knew they would never sit where they were told and so asked if she might photograph them. The Queen's diary secretary, Helen, duly emailed to say that 'Holly, Willow,

Vulcan and Candy would be happy to keep an appointment' on such and such a date.

When Nicky arrived at the Palace with her camera, she found the dogs in the care of a footman called Ian. The dogs clearly thought he was about to take them out for a walk, and were running around barking. It was complete chaos. The only one that would sit still for long enough was Vulcan, who seemed rather less athletic than the others; Holly was the worst: she would not keep still for a second, and all the photographs Nicky took of her were hopelessly blurred.

She asked Helen if she could come back, and two days later she met the dogs again and managed to get Vulcan. But Holly was still being impossible. She finally nailed her down at Windsor Castle, where she again met Ian. As they walked towards the rose garden, a car arrived with the dogs in the back, barking and leaping about 'like a whole lot of naughty schoolchildren'. The driver extracted Holly, put her on a lead and took her across to them. 'She was like a sulky teenager,' says Nicky, 'but she cheered up, and then I got some very sweet photos of her. She was adorable – they were all adorable – but noisy.'

Nicky Philipps divides her time between London and Picton Castle in Pembrokeshire, her former family home that is now open to the public and run by a trust. A couple of years after she painted the portrait, the Queen and the Duke of Edinburgh had lunch at the castle on a visit to Wales and Nicky was invited, too.

'Ma'am, you may remember Nicky,' said their host, from the trust. 'She painted you with the dogs.'

'No,' said the Queen. 'You painted me, and then the dogs!' Had she been miffed they were not there together – or is she just a stickler for accuracy?

There have not been many occasions when she has been painted with the dogs. But Michael Leonard, who painted her nearly three decades earlier in 1985, was keen to have a corgi from the outset – although his initial reaction to the commission from the *Reader's Digest* was lukewarm. 'I am flattered to be asked, Ken,' he told the art editor, at a private viewing, 'but quite honestly I have never had any ambition to paint the Queen. She is, after all, more of an icon than an individual. A searching likeness of an icon is surely a bit of a contradiction in terms—? It began to dawn on me, though, that here was an opportunity to go straight to the top of the social ladder in one bound without actually having to work my way up it! Fortified by another drink, I went back to Ken and said, "Look, Ken, forget what I said earlier – I'd be delighted to paint the Queen for you!'

The painting, which now hangs in the National Portrait Gallery, was to mark the Queen's sixtieth birthday. What he wanted was an informal picture with his subject in ordinary clothes and, to reinforce the relaxed atmosphere, he wanted a corgi. His mother had had a corgi so he knew the breed and knew precisely what it would bring to the portrait. He had a preliminary meeting at the Palace, his plans were okayed and he had a preview of the room where he would paint, to check the light.

The Yellow Drawing Room is specially set aside for portraits and has a chair set on a raised dais, which he rejected as being too formal. Michael was promised three hour-long sittings. The first was in June, on the afternoon of a gloomy, rainy day. Thanks to a formal lunch with a Chinese delegation going on far longer than expected, the Queen arrived 40 minutes late.

Michael had decided not to sketch or paint in the sittings but to concentrate on taking photographs and work from those. The light was fading fast and his nerves were escalating.

'I'm afraid the Chinese prime minister was rather talkative,' she said, sitting compliantly in the corner of the sofa he had selected. She was wearing duck-egg blue, and Spark, the corgi that had arrived with her, immediately jumped onto the sofa beside her and pushed her nose into her lap.

'This was exactly what I hoped would happen,' said Michael. 'It's what my mother's corgi used to do.' He had specifically asked for the best behaved of the dogs. 'Having the dog there made everything easier,' he says. 'I can't talk about horse flesh or anything else the Queen would be interested it; and chattering on isn't something the Queen does. But she loves her dogs and she was keeping Spark amused and keeping her lively.'

He was happy with the composition but he wanted the Queen to sit up very straight; her posture was not especially good. How to ask? He thought adjusting the dog might be the answer. 'Could you hoick her up a bit, ma'am?' he ventured. It worked a treat – but in the painting he did tweak her posture some more to make her taller, and scaled down Spark's size a little.

The second sitting was a month later and the Queen forgot to bring the dog, so while her private secretary, Sir William Heseltine, went off to find Spark, Michael showed her his photos from the first session and asked whether she would mind if he changed some of the colours to make the painting more harmonious: the carroty-gold of the corgi against the bright blue of her dress drew the eye too much, and he wanted her face to dominate the picture. He showed her a little colour study of what he had in mind, but she was so disinterested that in the end he did what he wanted without consulting anyone. He put her in yellow and sat her on soft pink damask.

'She looked with polite interest,' he says, 'but she was bored.' She had sat for dozens of portraits – it is now at least 129. At that time, a couple of hours were set aside for sittings most weeks that she was at Buckingham Palace.

Spark had been let out into the garden with the other dogs and while they awaited her arrival, he asked about the dog. 'She seems very good-natured, ma'am,' he ventured nervously.

'Well – not always,' said the Queen. 'Actually, Spark

is leader of the pack and together with the other dogs, has been known to harry the gardeners.'

'I'm rather glad I didn't know about this earlier, ma'am,' he said.

'Oh, she is very well-behaved on her own. Only, the other day, she and some of the others were rounding up a group of workers in the garden. They had taken their shirts off in the hot weather so were half-naked.' The more she spoke of the dog, the more animated she became – it was because of the dog that Michael was able to get the animation he craved into the portrait. As Nicky Philipps says, 'She's one of those people whose resting face is terrifying. They have these wonderful smiles but when they drop it, they have a face that looks as though it wants to knife you.'

When Spark finally arrived, hot and panting, she hopped straight up onto the sofa beside the Queen and sat dribbling profusely. 'It's just like having a hot-water bottle in your lap,' said the Queen as she wiped the big, dark blobs of saliva from her dress.

CHAPTER 14

Off Duty

Corgis and dorgis are undoubtedly the dogs that most people associate with the Queen, and rightly so: they have been her constant companions since the age of seven, and she has so often been seen with them. But there is another world that most urbanites know little or nothing about: the world of field sports. It is populated by people who pick up their Purdeys on the 'Glorious Twelfth' of August, when the grouse season starts, and blast their way through the autumn and winter months, through the duck, partridge, pheasant and wildfowl seasons, until it comes to an end in February – although rabbit and hare can be shot all year round. They do this on some of the biggest and most beautiful estates in the country, often paying thousands of pounds a day for the privilege. And standing not far behind them are people with dogs, which they send out to 'pick-up' the fallen quarry.

To those who have shot with the Queen in this world of flat hats, tweed, wellies and waxed rainwear, she is something of a pin-up; not because she is Queen, but because the stars of this world are the dogs. And she is an expert handler and one of the most experienced breeders of gundogs in the country. The kennels at Sandringham, where she still personally oversees the breeding programmes, have produced some of the best working dogs, including five famous field trial champions. These are competitions to test a dog's ability to be controlled from a distance by its handler in the field under the simulated conditions of a shoot. Nowhere, but nowhere, is she more in her element or more at ease than on a shoot. It is here, resembling a down-at-heel bag-lady, layered against the elements, that she truly comes to life. There is no need for feigned interest or forced conversation. Here she is the country woman amongst fellow country folk, using dogs for the purpose for which they were originally bred. She knows as much as there is to know about bloodlines and conformation, and has an encyclopaedic memory about the dogs she has bred. As she does the horses. She understands animals and that is the secret. And, as her head keeper, David Clark, says, 'The great thing is, animals understand her as well. That's why she's an amazing dog handler.'

Shooting, like all blood sports, is clearly a contentious issue. Its proponents say that because of it, millions of pounds go into management of the countryside and the environment to provide cover for game, from which a wide range of other species also benefit. They will point to many endangered species that are now thriving as a result, like curlew and lapwing. Without shooting, they say, that money would not be spent; the land would be barren and uniform. The sport also brings jobs to rural communities. Its adversaries say that it is cruel, unethical, and a large number of predators, some of which are protected, are killed by gamekeepers wanting to protect their game. They argue that it is out of keeping with modern views on animal welfare.

'Driven shoots' are perhaps the most inflammatory. The 'guns', of which there are usually eight or ten, with two shotguns per person, stand in a line at pegs – or in the case of grouse, which are cannier than other game birds, in camouflaged butts to avoid being spotted. Each one has someone who loads the guns for him by his side. Meanwhile, a collection of beaters and flankers advance on the guns, flushing the game out of its cover and steering it towards them, shouting, whistling and flapping arms and flags as they do so.

This is where most of the serious money is, and driven shoots have historically been the preserve of the aristocracy and the upper classes, although today the only qualification is money. There are also more women shooting these days, too. In the past the men shot and their womenfolk picked-up, which is to say, managed the dogs, and this is precisely what the Queen has done for Prince Philip at shoots all over the country throughout their marriage. She has never shot game herself.

'Rough shooting', otherwise known as 'walked up', or 'shooting over dogs', has always been more egalitarian, cheaper to do and seems to the outsider less like mass slaughter. There are no beaters and the guns are not in a fixed position; they send their dogs forward to hunt for game and flush out of hiding whatever they find. This is where spaniels, pointers and setters come into their own: they are better hunters than Labradors. But pointers and setters do what it says on the box: they find the game and stand and point at it, so people with pointers need a retriever for the picking-up. The Queen has never had pointers but she allows the Pointer Club to hold international field trial events on her land. The last one was at Balmoral in 2010, which she was not able to attend herself, but she made sure everyone was well looked after and sent Alan Goodship, who manages the Sandringham kennels, with a favourite yellow Labrador, Russet, to retrieve for them.

Whatever the rights and wrongs, the Queen has been involved in this world since she was a child. She has shot deer – as her mother did – but never game, probably because it was rare for women to use a shotgun when she was young. But, growing up, it was an everyday part of life that everyone she knew and associated with took part in, and had done for generations. She watched her father and his friends shooting and saw how skilfully the dogs were worked. She longed to get involved, and commandeered any available dog to find birds at Balmoral, including the corgis; but George VI did not think it fitting for princesses to pick-up. It was her first gundog trainer, Jack Curtis, who finally encouraged her to handle a Labrador, and it turned out she had a real flair for it.

Most gundogs in this specialist world have pedigrees that are often even more impressive and blue-blooded than their owners'. And those dogs can open doors that their owners never could without them. As Janet Menzies, a writer but also a breeder and trainer in Somerset with five field trial champions to her name, explains: 'I'm just a girl from Toxteth, I'm not posh or anything like that, but because my dogs are posh I get invites like you wouldn't believe: Lord This is saying, "Jan, have you got any puppies?" and the Duchess of That is saying, "Do you realise that your puppy must therefore be the great-niece of Teal? You must bring her up shooting." In this world it's possible for the Queen to be herself and that's really important, it is something she must relish. In Labradors, she had Sandringham Sydney that everyone talks about, handled for her by Bill Meldrum. No matter who owned that dog it was one of the best retrievers of its generation in its own right. And that was nothing to do with it being the Queen's dog whatsoever.'

The Queen's first personal gundogs in the 1960s were Snare and Sabre, both black Labradors; they were later joined by Wren, who was also black. She loved them, as every photograph and clip of old film of them together attests. She has had a wonderful relationship with all of her working dogs, but they were not pets. As one of the Sandringham keepers remembered, 'She doesn't put up with any nonsense from them and if they were going to be a bit wayward she would deal with them on the spot, how they should be dealt with.' They lived in the kennels at Sandringham, and while they may have loved the Queen above all others, and joined the corgis and dorgis on walks, they were looked after with all the other gundogs by kennel staff, and would never have slept in the house. Some gundogs, also dearly loved, are never even brought into the house. They are more relaxed in their own space. 'They're like teenage girls,' says Janet, 'preferring to be left alone to do their own thing in their bedrooms.'

Labradors originated not in Labrador as the name might suggest, but in Newfoundland, where they worked with fishermen and were known as St John's dogs. They had a broad head, thick double coat and short otter tail, and were first brought to the United Kingdom in the 1830s, by two British aristocrats, the 2nd Earl of Malmesbury and the 5th Duke of Buccleuch. What they had admired in these dogs was their temperament and their love of water and retrieving.

Both men set up breeding kennels: the earl, on the south coast, used them for wildfowling, while the duke worked them as gundogs in the Scottish Borders. A generation later, in the early 1880s, the 3rd Earl of Malmesbury and the 6th Duke of Buccleuch met out shooting and agreed to breed their respective dogs. The first two entries in the *Stud Book of the Duke of Buccleuch Labrador Retrievers* were the gifts made by Lord Malmesbury to the 6th Duke.

All Buccleuch Labradors can be traced back to those

first imported dogs, which makes them almost unique in their purity; and although numbers dwindled some years ago, they are now safely on the rise again after the 10th Duke, Richard Buccleuch, brought in a new gundog manager, David Lisett, to restore them. If there is a 'first family' of the canine world, the duke's Labradors must surely be it. Although Sandringham Labradors are not far behind them.

The Queen is nothing if not competitive and the more she worked her dogs, the more she wanted to improve the bloodlines, build up the Sandringham name and enter their best dogs for field trials. So, after Jack Curtis retired in 1964, she approached a likeable young Scot called Bill Meldrum as his replacement. Bill had been working as a keeper, having started his career at the age of 15 under his father, George, who was a keeper at Leslie House in Fife. His father trained gundogs and ran them successfully in field trials, and Bill followed suit.

'Like anything,' he told *Shooting Times* in 2009, 'I enjoyed doing it [field trialling] simply for the sport and then all of a sudden I got two very good dogs and was very successful with them. I made up both dogs to field trial champions and in one year came second with the bitch at the Championship, and third the next year. The Championship was at Sandringham and the Queen was spectating. She came over and asked me how I trained my dogs. It was the first time I met her, and she was very interested in the gundogs.'

The following year, 1963, he won the Championship at Woburn Abbey with Glenfarg Skid, one of several Labradors owned by Mrs Harcourt-Wood, which his father looked after and trained for her. Not long afterwards Bill had a phone call from the Queen's land agent, Captain William Fellowes, (the father of Lord Robert Fellowes, who was the Queen's private secretary for many years). Would he and his wife like to come and spend a few days at Sandringham?

'They put us up in a hotel, showed us round, then Captain Fellowes took us up to meet the Queen, and we talked away in the ballroom. She told me that it was her ambition to own a field trial champion. I thought, "I'm only a gamekeeper in my twenties and here's the Queen talking to me about gundogs." I was completely taken aback when she then asked me if I'd like to come and work for her.'

Initially, when they saw the house that went with the job, the Meldrums turned the offer down. But the Duke of Edinburgh, with typical decisiveness, interceded on their behalf, telling Fellowes: 'You'll have to do that house up, you can't ask people to go and live in a house like that.' He then turned to the young couple and said, 'If we do the house up to your liking, would you consider it?'

'So we came to Sandringham,' said Bill, 'with the intention of staying only for a short time. We'd moved around a bit and I wasn't sure if I wanted to train the dogs full-time, so I said to the Queen that we'd stay for four or five years. When I went for my twenty-year medal, I walked into the room and she had a big smile on her face and said to me, "I knew that for someone who said they'd only stay for four or five years, once you got here you'd never leave."

'It is a wonderful estate to be on and the Queen is a wonderful person. She was always totally 100 per cent interested in the dogs. I never bred a bitch without discussing it with her. She always had the final say. We got on great together.'

After 20 years working the Queen's dogs, the Duke

of Edinburgh, who has always run the shooting on all the estates, asked him if he would like to be head keeper, and for the next 21 years he did the two jobs together. He still lives, in retirement, with his wife in a cottage on the Sandringham estate. He has a very special relationship with the Queen, just as Bill Fenwick did for all those years at Windsor, and has known the side of her that so few people have truly known. He has friends all over. 'One of the finest men you could ever meet,' said one, echoing many others. 'The Queen loved him and calls on him when she is in residence. He tells wonderful stories – at his retirement dinner at Windsor, people were crying with laughter.'

Sandringham was bought for the future Edward VII when he was 21, in 1862. He loved the place, made it his home and frequently filled it with friends. He transformed the shooting on the estate into some of the best in the county, building the kennels in 1879. They were made out of brick and local carrstone, and housed up to a hundred dogs: each had a run, enclosed with iron railings, and there was a large paddock for exercise.

He began the Sandringham strain of black Labradors in 1911 but while he was a passionate shot, he was never as good at the sport as his eldest son. When George V came to the throne, he let his widowed mother, Alexandra, continue to keep her dogs in the kennels at Sandringham and started a breeding programme of his own at kennels nearby, under the Wolferton affix. After her death 15 years later, he switched the affix to Sandringham and re-introduced the Clumber spaniel that his father had favoured. Being bigger and heavier than other spaniels, they were particularly good in the bracken that grows in abundance at Sandringham. 'A Clumber,' Edward once said, 'could do the work of three beaters.'

The only time the kennels were without dogs in nearly 90 years was during Edward VIII's brief reign, when he closed them down when he saw how much they cost. The Queen's father reopened them and, in 1949, brought a Labrador called Windsor Bob into the kennels who had famously won the Kennel Club Retriever Trials the previous year. He helped improve the Sandringham strain, and after her father's death, the Queen carried on his breeding programme. What interested her most of all was working the dogs from a distance, and that was why she had been so attracted to the friendly young Scot from Fife.

CHAPTER 15

Sydney and Co.

For all their Edwardian splendour, the Sandringham kennels had been neglected and were in a state of disrepair when Bill Meldrum arrived. Shortly afterwards, there was a change of guard: the captain retired as land agent and was replaced by Sir Julian Lloyd.

Money was tight and a decision was taken that it was cheaper to replace than restore. Over a two-year period, the old kennels were demolished and new modern, wooden kennels with welded mesh runs were built. And it was in those kennels – which can house around 40 dogs – that the Queen and Bill went on to breed some legendary names.

The Queen's three personal Labradors were good hunting dogs, ideal for picking-up, but she wanted a dog that could be handled from 200 yards away; she wanted a field trial champion, and that was what Bill set about helping her achieve.

The first success came with a bitch named Sherry of Biteabout, bred by Bill Davidson, an electrician from Durham. Sherry arrived at Sandringham in July 1964. Her sire was Glenfarg Skid. Sherry became very dear to the Queen's heart. 'I would say Sherry was the Queen's favourite,' Meldrum told *The Field*. 'Sherry was a star.'

Bill Davidson was a good friend of the other Bill and over the years he became a trusted friend to the Queen too; he trained and handled some of her dogs and was always impressed by how knowledgeable she was. They corresponded. In his excitement, he framed the first handwritten letter he had from her, but by the end, the letters were simply stacked in a box and no one knew he had them. The Queen was so fond of him she gave him a dorgi named Sharpy, which lived to the age of

11. Tragically, one day, when Bill was away judging a competition in Northern Ireland, the dog dug himself out of his kennel and was run over.

The Queen wanted to replace him but Bill was not well enough to have a new dog. He had asbestosis and died of leukaemia the week before his 74th birthday in 2001. Before he died, he willed the Biteabout affix to his good friend and fellow breeder and field trial judge, Malcolm Taylor, and the name lives on.

Bill Meldrum made Sherry up into a field trial champion (in other words, trained her to the highest level) and then gave her to the Queen to handle. There are people in the gundog world who still talk about the day she made a memorable retrieve with Sherry. The story goes that a grouse at Balmoral that had been hit continued flying into the distance, before collapsing and dying on a tumulus of heather raised like a table above the surrounding moor. As the late John Humphreys wrote in *Country Life*, 'It was a long retrieve [estimated at 800 yards], and time and again, the Queen got the dog to the area, but, as it had flushed a live grouse from the same spot, she had difficulty persuading the dog to keep hunting on the peat hag. She was so involved she didn't realise the drive had ended and that the shooting party had gathered behind her.

Bill Davidson with Sandringham Mango

'At last, Sherry hit the scent, picked the bird and came galloping back. There was a spatter of applause and the Queen was overcome with embarrassment, saying that she could never have done that had she known all those people were watching.'

She and Bill used to train together. 'She got to be very

good at it,' he says. 'She had picked up a lot from watching field trials. Yes, I gave her some advice – and she gave me some too!' Once he had made the dogs up, the Queen ran them in private trials that Bill organised at Sandringham. They were held every year during the last week in April, and eight of the best handlers in the country would be invited to compete. One year she won it with a dog called Sandringham Brae. After her run, the Queen went over to check out the score board, which had not yet revealed the winning places. A couple of the other handlers were standing next to her, and in her headscarf, coat and wellies, had not realised who was beside them. 'We know who's won today,' one said to the other. 'The Queen. Her dogs are a mile in front.' In recounting the story to Bill, the Queen said, 'That made me feel very good.' When Brae came to the end of his days, it was he who was buried alongside the others in the pet cemetery with his headstone bearing the legend, 'A Gentleman Amongst Dogs.'

For all her skill, the Queen never took part in public trials. Breeder and trainer Janet Menzies understands that – as do most owners, from the Duchess of Devonshire to the Duke of Buccleuch. 'We all have professional handlers who do it for us because we are so bloody nervous we can't manage it ourselves,' says Janet. 'We are all really involved with our dogs but when it comes to the top competitions . . . It's like owning a racehorse – you don't attempt to ride it yourself in the Cheltenham Gold Cup, you hire a professional jockey.'

'The Queen left me alone for three months,' said Bill Meldrum of his early days in the job, 'and I spotted a very good bitch in the kennels, which I liked and which had breeding that I liked. She came from the Duke of Wellington's estate as a present. Her name was Sandringham Juniper [bred by the Marquess of Douro], and I suggested to the Queen that we bred her with Skid, my dog that had won the Championship the year before. She agreed to it and we had a litter of puppies out of her, and we had quite a lot of success after that.'

The puppies were called Sandringham Pan, Sharp, Skate, Skid, Sled, Slipper and Sloe. Of those, Sandringham Slipper, a black bitch, became a field trial champion, one of the Queen's best and most successful competitive dogs; and although she did not keep Skid's daughter, Sandringham Magpie, Magpie also went on to become a champion.

The Queen has personally named all her dogs, of every breed, which, given the hundreds of dogs she has bred over the years, is a feat in itself, although in fairness, some have been repeated – and there is always a theme. She has named them after flowers, islands, birds, drinks, trees, metals, makes of car and fictional characters from favourite books. Sometimes they all started with the same letter of the alphabet. In the case of Sherry's son, Sandringham Sydney, he was so called because she was in Australia in 1970 when he was born, so the whole litter were named after Australian landmarks.

The Duke of Edinburgh had his own dogs, Labradors, which he named himself, but he had a very different outlook. He only ever kept two dogs and he wanted nothing more ambitious from them than that they should retrieve from a maximum of 30 metres. His relationship with his dogs was nothing like the Queen's was with hers, and he had little understanding of her obsession. His interest was in the shooting and management and conservation of the land.

The Queen's beloved Sherry died in February 1978 and was immortalised in the Sandringham cemetery as another 'Faithful companion of the Queen.' But her line lived on. Sydney, who was yellow, went on to become the Queen's most celebrated dog – the most famous and unforgettable of the Sandringham Labradors. He won the coveted CLA Trophy at the Game Fair in 1972, 1974 and 1975, competing against the top 12 gundogs in the country, a record that has never been equalled. He was also a prolific breeder. He mated 77 bitches in one year alone. His yellow son, Sandringham Salt, born the year Sherry died, was another champion. But disappointingly, Sydney was never the Queen's closest companion. He proved to be more of a man's dog.

As Bill Meldrum once said of him: 'Sydney was a showman. He loved the crowds. Once he had become a champion the Queen took over handling him, but he was a bit of a character and liked to do his own thing.' The Queen told Bill that Sydney was just using her to get him to and from the shoot. She said, 'Sydney looks at me as if to say, "You be here with the Land Rover to collect me at the end of the drive."'

At that time they were breeding an average of six

litters a year, from sires and bitches that the Queen would personally inspect and select. They were usually born between April and the end of May, and from those they kept 15 for training, which would begin in February of the following year when the puppies were nine to ten months old. They were looking for 'a bold puppy with a nice head, nice tail and thick-set legs; and a nice nature,' says Annie Meldrum, who puppy-walked and was a part of the selection process. By July they would narrow it down to five and the rest were sold as half-trained dogs, but never as pets – always to shooting people as working dogs.

Bill Meldrum always aimed for the bitches to whelp in the spring so that they were a reasonable size when the dogs all migrated to Balmoral in August, along with the Queen, Prince Philip and other members of the royal family, who would all come with their dogs too. The dogs spent ten weeks in Scotland 'for the grouse' – as they still do today – travelling through the night in a specially adapted lorry with two drivers and a kennel boy. Bill would usually take up about 30 to have some in reserve and to give them a holiday.

The grouse shooting at Balmoral is amongst the best,

and this is where the dogs do some of their hardest work. The moors, where the grouse live, cover a huge area, and by August the heather is a good two feet high and tough going for man, woman and beast. The beaters start their advance from up to two miles away. 'It's like watching an army appear on the horizon,' says Janet Menzies. 'Like a scene from *Zulu*. And then the birds come [doing up to 70 mph] and they're like a Spitfire squadron, and you're a bit scared, which is silly because they are fluffy birds and you have two socking great guns and a load of cartridges.'

Bill Meldrum always looked forward to running the young dogs on the hill. 'A trainer always wants young dogs, it's more exciting,' he said. 'Within the kennels we had purely picking-up dogs and I would keep about four or five field trialling dogs as well, which would go with me on the hill, but they would only get special retrieves.' Once north of the border, the dogs earned their keep. 'If I didn't go to Balmoral with at least twenty-two dogs, I was in trouble. They had to have a rest. Some keepers take their dogs every day on the hill but after two days the dogs get careless. If I saw a dog getting careless I dropped him off and let him have a couple of days' rest.

When dogs get tired you don't get the same out of them and they make mistakes.'

After ten weeks in the heather, the lorry took its precious cargo south again for the partridges and duck at Sandringham, then back up to Balmoral in October for more grouse – if stocks were holding up – then back to Sandringham for pheasants and partridges. During that time the Queen would collect four dogs from the kennels on the morning of a shoot day, and, having loaded them into the back of her Range Rover, would join the picking-up team. 'She was, and still is in my opinion, a very good handler who has a great knowledge of what a dog should do,' he said.

Bill Meldrum handed over the kennel keys after 41 years to Alan Goodship and his wife Lynda – both corgi-lovers. Alan was the fourth generation in his family to work on the Sandringham estate, having started out puppy-walking for Bill when he was a twelve-year-old schoolboy. He had then been a beat keeper [a game keeper in charge of a particular section of a shoot] for more than 30 years. He knew the place, the people and the pooches through and through. 'Mr Meldrum taught me standards,' he told *The Field*. 'He was fair; you never did anything he didn't do. He and Mrs Meldrum were both very kind to me.'

By the time he took over, the trialling days were over. 'We were successful in the sixties and seventies,' says Bill, 'but after I became head keeper as well, it fell off. I didn't have time for the trials.' This suited Goodship down to the ground. 'Mr Meldrum was never at home,' he has since said, with a grin. 'I don't travel. I'm a Norfolk boy. My country stops at King's Lynn.' So apart from the annual trips to Balmoral, he concentrates on training the dogs and being a member of the picking-up team on shoot days. Not to mention that the dogs need to be fed morning and evening, and exercised three or four times a day.

But the peripatetic life had been productive. By the time Bill Meldrum hung up his whistle, he had provided the Queen with five field trial champions.

CHAPTER 16

Playing Host

The Kennel Club divides breeds into seven categories: Gundog, Hound, Pastoral, Terrier, Toy, Utility and Working. These are based on what the dog was originally bred for, but the majority of all breeds these days, even the working ones, are owned as pets – more Labradors are to be found snuggling on sofas than running around with dead pheasants in their mouths, and some are being specifically bred for the show ring. But amongst the shooting fraternity, the mark of a good dog is to have a field trial champion (FTCh) in its pedigree, which is why the Queen was so keen to up the game at Sandringham. Breeders can charge premium prices – just as they can if there is a Crufts winner in the family tree.

There are field trial championships for the various classes of gundogs: Labrador retrievers retrieve; spaniels flush and retrieve; pointers and setters hunt, and freeze on point when scenting game. The trials are the pinnacle of the working dog world, hosted by landowners with large estates – like the Duke of Buccleuch on his Queensberry estate in the Scottish Borders, the Duke of Westminster at Abbeystead in Lancashire, Lord Vestey at Stowell Park in Gloucestershire, Lord Percy at Alnwick in Northumberland and the Duchess of Devonshire at Chatsworth in Derbyshire – people who so love dogs they are prepared to set aside ground and game, and forfeit the income from two or three days' shooting at the height of the season.

The Queen has played host many times over many years, at Windsor, Sandringham and Balmoral; most recently it was to the 2018 Cocker Spaniel Championships at Sandringham – for the seventh time since their inception in 1993. Her shoots are not commercial; never-theless, a year's worth of preparation goes into hosting these events, and a lot of game needs to be available. The organisation of this latest event fell to the head keeper, David Clark, who retired shortly afterwards and admits his swan song was a challenge. 'It's a nightmare!' he told Janet Menzies, who reported on the day for *The Field*. 'Her Majesty agreed to hold the Championship more than a year ago and that's when we started preparations. They are all wild birds, and one of the problems we had today is that the birds were running along in front of us. There is a massive attendance at an event like this, so with a couple of hundred people walking along watching, that's an added difficulty. It is a relief to get the two days done successfully, and my team worked so hard behind the scenes to make sure the birds were there. I think Her Majesty enjoyed it – she came out and stayed out in the line on both days, so I think she was finding it exciting.' Richard Buccleuch encapsulates, I suspect, what the Queen and every other host feels, and why, despite the stresses, they host again and again. Speaking to Janet Menzies, he said, '. . . in the training of dogs, I am captured by the passion and enthusiasm we all have. If it wasn't for that, a hard head might say, "What are we doing?" But you get carried away, and I see all these wonderful competitors who love their dogs and give their all and we are all swept away by the excitement. I feel exhilarated by the tension and excitement and the incredible skill shown by both handlers and dogs. It makes it a privilege to have these people here.'

The Sovereign in her element

These are treasured occasions for people who would never normally be invited onto the Queen's land or get to meet her. But as fellow dog handlers, they have the opportunity to work their dogs over some of the best shooting country in the British Isles and they appreciate her trust and her generosity. Security is very low-key on these days, but as Janet Menzies says, 'The Queen's best security is to be loved. And when she is on her turf with her people, she's got three hundred pairs of eyes looking out for her and if we noticed anybody who didn't look quite right that would be sorted out.'

Just three months short of her 92nd birthday, on a raw January day, the Queen not only drove herself up to the line in her Range Rover, she walked with the competitors for two hours on both days across heather and thick, flat bracken, leaving many younger than her struggling to keep up. Jon Kean, the Scottish chairman of the Kennel Club's Cocker Championship Working Party, walked with her on both days and was impressed. 'The Queen has vast experience with retrievers and cockers and I think it was wonderful she was able to attend both days. She was really impressed with the standard of the working cockers. She is so knowledge-able, and very perceptive in her comments.'

Janet Menzies has encountered the Queen on several occasions and even once trodden on her toe. She says that the Queen's love of gundogs puts her on an equal footing with her subjects that she rarely experiences elsewhere. 'If she's working a dog alongside another woman who is working her dog, they are equals, and when you meet the Queen under those circumstances that's what comes across very strongly – and how relaxed and happy she is. And she's actually not your queen, she's like your aunt, working a gundog and you can talk about gundogs. I think for her that must be the most wonderful world, because it's something she's really interested in. It's her true self.' As her head keeper, David Clark, has said, 'You see a lady wearing a headscarf with a load of dogs around her, and in a field of sporting people you wouldn't pick Her Majesty out.'

Janet's bitch, FTCh Gourneycourt Morag, aka Fudge (because of her colour), was competing in the Cocker Championships at Sandringham in 2008, being handled by her friend and fellow trainer, Jonathan Bailey. The little dog was in what's called the 'run-off', which is the final round of the competition where the best dogs are invited to go forward to determine where they will be placed. As her owner and trainer, Janet went forward with her handler for this final test.

'The run is basically a simulated rough-shooting day,' explains Janet, 'so there are guns either side of you who will shoot any bird that is flushed by the dog and the dog hunts in front of you and it must be steady and must hunt, quickly, effectively and efficiently and it must have no faults, e.g. chasing or making a noise. The major fault would be chasing because it becomes impossible for the gun to shoot the bird if the dog's in the way, particularly if it were a rabbit or something like that. So the minute the dog has a find, it either flushes it into the air, or bolts it if it's a rabbit, but the dog must stop the minute it's done that, and be perfectly still so the shooting can be done safely. Then when it's shot they go and retrieve the bird and bring it back to you.

'I was terribly nervous. Fudge was doing great and the judges said that was that; and I turned round to walk out of the line and into the gallery of spectators and as I did I brushed into someone and trod on their toe. I turned round and – the Queen is so tiny! I thought, "S***, this is the Queen!" Which gave me a huge dilemma because you are not allowed to speak to Her Majesty until you've been presented, but obviously I can't hang around waiting to be presented in order to apologise. Plus I've been to garden parties and met the Queen under more formal circumstances and you curtsey, don't you? I was wearing wellies, breeches, and over the top of it, waterproof over-trousers, and then a tweed coat. So essentially I looked like Compo off *Last of the Summer Wine*, and trying to curtsey, plucking at my waterproof trousers.

'As I was doing all of this I thought the Queen must think we are all absolute raving lunatics. Here I am mouth flapping, bobbing up and down in front of her and she just said, "Is that your little dog?" And I said, "Yes, Your Majesty," and she said, "Oh, I do like her so much, she's working very well, isn't she? But she's so small I could hardly see her." I replied, "Yes, but she's speedy . . ."'

'We were in the middle of this conversation when Prince Philip walked over and elbowed me and said, "You ought to get a black one, that would be much easier to see." And the Queen threw him a look which said, "Philip knows nothing about this!"

'That was not an interaction with the Queen, it was

an interaction with the host of the trial or a fellow dog lady. I never did get the chance to apologise about her toe, but she wasn't bothered at all.'

The next time they met, the Queen immediately said, 'Oh, yes, I remember your dog, that lovely little brown one,' and gave her a beaming smile.

Thanks to Sydney and co., Sandringham Labradors became highly sought after and the Sandringham affix is still seen in all the best bloodlines. But alongside the Labs, which the Queen once said she bred because it was the 'normal thing to do', by the mid-1970s, she had become interested in cocker spaniels, and with Bill Meldrum set about breeding them. 'The Queen was very much ahead of her time in her appreciation of the charismatic cocker,' says Janet Menzies. 'In the 1980s they were a bit of a trialling afterthought, bred and handled by just a small coterie of mainly professionals who regarded cocker trials as a bit of fun and relaxation from "serious" gundogs. Today it's cockers that get talked about, with a massive influx of new breeders, trainers and owners.' Modern cockers have lost their reputation for being 'devil dogs' that are inconsistent and difficult to train, although devotees still relish their free spirit. 'Cockers are like racehorses,' says one, 'and when they are fit and competing they are going to be quite tricky to handle. It can be hard to get them settled, but you want that drive – they should always be an exciting breed to watch.'

While the Queen has only had a handful of them, she has had success. She started with a bitch called Isherwood Medlar, who came through Bill Davidson. His dog, Toffee of Biteabout, sired Medlar. She arrived in the kennels at the end of 1975 and her son, Sandringham Mango – from her first litter, whom the Queen gave to her racing manager, Henry Porchester, 7th Earl of Carnarvon – went on to became a field trial champion in 1981, handled by Bill Davidson. The Queen kept her other son, Maxwell, who never won any great trials but was special in another respect: a little girl had written to the Queen to say that she knew Her Majesty liked dogs and thought that Maxwell would be a good name for one of them. The Queen wrote back thanking the little girl and said that when she next had a litter of puppies she would take her advice and call one of them Maxwell.

The man who trains and runs the Queen's dogs today is Ian Openshaw, a professional and legendary figure in the gundog world, who won his first Kennel Club open qualifier at the age of 15. After 12 years as a pheasant keeper, he set up Rytex Gundogs near Market Drayton in Shropshire 20 years ago with his wife, Wendy, and the business has gone from strength to strength. Now in his fifties, he has made up over a hundred champions – with Labrador retrievers, cockers and springers – and set a record that is unlikely to be beaten. One of those dogs is a black cocker spaniel he bred called Mallowdale Diamond, which is owned by the Queen. Diamond was presented to the Queen as a tiny puppy by the Kennel Club at Sandringham in 2013, as a thank-you for hosting the championships that January. In 2015 Diamond won the Yorkshire gundog open qualifiers; the next year she won the Kennel Club open qualifiers; and in 2017 Ian ran her at the cocker championships at the Duke of Westminster's Abbeystead estate in Lancashire. She had a litter of puppies that same year under the Wolferton kennel name: Dawn, Domino, Drama and Dynasty, so further success may yet be to come.

Alas, Diamond's success has prompted controversy.

A group on Facebook, calling themselves 'Proper Cockers', have accused Ian Openshaw of cross-breeding springer spaniels with cockers and producing what is known as a 'sprocker', to get a stronger, faster dog. 'It's like racing a six-cylinder car in a four-cylinder race,' said one. 'Cockers can't compete with them.' And sprockers, being cross-breeds, are disqualified from competing in Kennel Club field trials. The group claim that Mallowdale Diamond is one of these imposters. Inevitably, it has been dubbed 'Cockergate'. I fear there will be no definitive resolution.

The whole incident has upset the trialling community and, no doubt, the Queen too. The phrase 'red in tooth and claw', it would seem, extends way beyond the animal world.

CHAPTER 17

A Change of Guard

While the corgi's long reign at Buckingham Palace may
be drawing to a close, there is no doubt that dogs of one
sort of another will roam around the royal corridors of
the future. The Queen may have failed to convince her
four children that corgis are the best breed to have as
pets, but she successfully brought them up to be confirmed
dog-lovers, and both Prince Charles and Prince William
– first and second in line to the throne respectively and
therefore the ones who will eventually inhabit those

corridors themselves – have never been without a four-footed friend. And neither has Prince George, currently third in line. In photographs released on his third birthday in 2016, he was seen offering to share his white chocolate ice-cream with Lupo, the family cocker spaniel.

The RSPCA immediately issued warnings that ice-cream and chocolate are both serious no-nos for dogs, but they missed the bigger picture. What greater love than that a three-year-old should give up his Magnum for a dog?

Prince Charles declared at an early age that he preferred Labradors to corgis, without specifying a reason. A clue may be in Prince Harry's comments when describing how well Meghan Markle had got on with the Queen when they first met. They had instantly bonded over the dogs. Speaking at their engagement interview in November 2017, he said that when he had first introduced Meghan to his grandmother, the dogs had taken to her straight away.

'I've spent the last thirty-three years being barked at,' he joked. 'This one walks in, absolutely nothing . . .'

'Just lying on my feet during tea,' said Meghan in confirmation. 'It was very sweet.'

'Just wagging tails, and I was just like, ugh!'

Meghan had two dogs when she was living as an actress in Toronto: Bogart, a crossbreed, and Guy, a beagle, who had been just days away from being put down in 2016, when she adopted him from a rescue home as a companion for Bogart. Bogart was too old to bring to London, so friends took him in, but she brought Guy, who has gone up in the world and is now happily installed in Nottingham Cottage, at Kensington Palace, and a close neighbour of Lupo. Lupo divides his time between Apartment 1A and Anmer Hall, the Duke and Duchess of Cambridge's home in Norfolk. He also frequently goes to stay with Kate's parents, Michael and Carole Middleton, in Berkshire. He is the son of their much-loved family dog, Ella.

Before Lupo, William had for many years a black Labrador called Wigeon, who doubled up as a gundog. William has inherited his grandmother's love of shooting and like his father and grandfather, he is a good shot. As is Harry. Hence the gasps of disbelief in December 2017 when Harry decided not to join the family on the traditional Boxing Day shoot at Sandringham. He had been an enthusiastic participant since the age of 12, but

Meghan, then his fiancée (until their marriage in May), disapproves of blood sports and so he stayed away.

For many years Prince Charles had a yellow Labrador called Harvey that went everywhere with him. Diana was no great dog-lover, however, and although she was not against shooting, she never took to Harvey, so Charles gave him away shortly after their marriage and switched his allegiance to Jack Russells, which he has had ever since. They are a small, combative crossbreed that also bark a lot, but are very popular, particularly amongst the hunting fraternity. In the days when fox hunting was legal, they would be used to go after foxes that escaped the hounds and went to ground. Tigga, his first, was a gift from Lady Salisbury, a friend who helped the Prince create the garden he so loves at Highgrove.

Tigga lived to the age of 18 and was the Prince's constant companion. For several years he also had Pooh, who was Tigga's daughter, until, to his huge distress, she disappeared when Charles was out walking with the dogs in woodland at Balmoral in April 1994. Despite a wide-ranging search, and the publication of a small ad in the local paper offering a reward for her safe return – which elicited an unlikely 'sighting' in Maida

Vale in north-west London – she was never seen again. It was generally assumed that she must have been lost down a rabbit hole.

To keep Tigga company, Camilla Parker Bowles, as she then was (now, since 2005, Duchess of Cornwall), gave Charles her own Jack Russell, Freddy, who was Pooh's brother and had been a gift as a puppy from the prince. Freddy then fathered a litter from which Charles took a bitch called Tosca. Sadly, Tosca and Tigga didn't get on, and so Tosca went to Camilla.

Camilla is another life-long dog-lover. She grew up with Sealyham terriers and, when married to Andrew Parker Bowles, they had both Sealyhams and Labradors. They also had a couple of corgis during the 1980s that were gifts from the Queen. Her current dogs are two Jack Russells, Beth and Bluebell, that she rescued from Battersea Dogs and Cats Home, of which she is now patron (it was one of the patronages that the Queen relinquished in 2016). Camilla had been a supporter of the charity for many years and prior to becoming patron, in 2010 she had been invited to open the new cattery at Battersea's main site under the arches of Chelsea Bridge. 'We knew she was a Jack Russell fan,' says Claire Horton, the chief executive, 'and she shared with us that she had lost her old Jack Russell, Freddy, a couple of years before. You can't come here and say, "I suppose I'll get another one at some point; I do miss having Freddy around," because we'll be watching for the right animal and as soon as one arrives we'll call you! We had a little puppy called Beth come in – she'd been abandoned. She was exactly what the Duchess was looking for, a really nice little dog, so we rang up and said, "What do you think?" I think she was at Balmoral. "Send me photos, send me photos!"' Beth joined Tosca and Rosie and settled in very happily.

The following year Bluebell was found dumped in a park. She was just four weeks old and was starving, shivering and suffering from a skin condition that had made her almost completely bald. She spent several weeks at Battersea while they tried to rehabilitate her. 'The Duchess said, "I'll definitely have her,"' says Claire. 'A couple of weeks later the dogs were having a few squabbles and we panicked because we thought we'd sent her a Chihuahua-cross, and they can be a bit feisty. "I'm not sure if it's a Chihuahua or a Jack Russell or what," the Duchess said, "but don't worry, we're persevering. She's not coming back."'

It was the mutual love of dogs (and horses) that, I have no doubt – despite all the years of scandal and heartache – helped cement the Queen's affection for her daughter-in-law, and which carries on to the next generation. One of the memorable events during the Diamond Jubilee year, in 2012, was when the Queen, Camilla and Kate – three generations of royal dog-lovers – all visited Fortnum and Mason together and discovered, to their delight, that in each of the hampers with which they were presented were dog biscuits.

Tail End

As Lady Pamela Hicks once said, 'The Queen is a very private person; a loner. She longs to be in a room with nobody else. The dogs, the horses, her husband . . . She has few friends and if she had to choose between the dogs, the horses and the friends, there is no doubt which she would choose.'

She has had a very special relationship with all her dogs, both the pets and the gundogs. But perhaps what is most interesting is that the relationship has always been two-way. So many of us dote on our dogs and our dogs, frankly, take the mickey out of us. However many training classes we take them to, they listen when it suits them and if something more interesting appears, they zone out and do their own sweet thing. Remember the video of Fenton the black Labrador in Richmond Park that went viral? His owner running after him bellowing 'Fenton! Fenton! Fenton! Oh, Jesus Christ!' as the dog disappears into the distance in hot pursuit of a herd of deer? It had several million views on YouTube and touched a nerve, I am sure, with the vast majority of amateur dog owners. 'There but for the grace of God,' we thought, 'go all of us.'

Whether the Queen would have identified with the situation, I cannot say, but I am sure it will have made her laugh. As Roger Mugford said, barely anyone on the planet can achieve the control over their dogs that the Queen can. And that comes from mutual respect, as well as love. One of her prime ministers at his weekly audience, surrounded by the dogs, once asked her how she could tell the difference between them all. 'Do you get your children confused?' was the clipped response.

According to Bill Meldrum, everyone at Sandringham

knows immediately when the Queen arrives, because the gundogs alert them. 'All the dogs in the kennels start barking the moment her car reaches the gate — it's a good 400 or 500 yards from the house. We have no idea how they can tell and they don't do that with anyone else.'

It brings to mind a story about the homecoming of another monarch: Odysseus, the King of Ithaca, in Homer's *Odyssey*. It describes his return after the ten-year siege of Troy and ten more years of hardship. He is with a friend and disguised as a beggar, so gaunt and ragged that no one, except his old dog Argos, recognises him.

The old hound is at death's door, lying outside the gate to the palace amid the dung of mules and cattle, covered in ticks and fleas. As his master approaches he lifts his head and pricks up his ears, then wags his tail and flattens his ears. That is all he can do; he is too weak to move.

Odysseus is momentarily overcome. He wipes a tear from his cheek and he has to look away to avoid his companion seeing. How could such a noble-looking dog be lying on a dung heap, he asks? The swineherd Eumaeus explains that the hound belonged to a man who died far away. 'If he were now what he used to be when Odysseus left and sailed off to Troy you would be astonished at his power and speed,' he says. 'No animal could escape him in the deep forest once he began to track it. What an amazing nose he had!'

The two men then go into the palace, and then the story continues: 'But Argos passed into the darkness of death, now that he had fulfilled his destiny of faith and seen his master once more after twenty years.'

Luckily, the Queen and her faithful companions have had altogether better luck. She has never suffered the deprivations Odysseus did, but she has shown the same unswerving loyalty to her country and inspired the same admiration and affection from her people. And it is her love of dogs, as much as anything else, that enables so many of us to feel we have a special connection with her. Strip away the wealth, the privilege and the palaces, and the bond she has with her dogs is no different from the bond the rest of us have with ours, no matter what our station in life.

And I am sure that, like the rest of us, she would agree with the late American actor, Will Rogers, who famously said, 'If there are no dogs in Heaven, then when I die I want to go where they went.'

Acknowledgements

First and foremost, I would like to thank Maddy Price, whose idea this book was, for asking me to write it. She has been a complete joy to work with, as are her colleagues, Rupert Lancaster and Kerry Hood; and great thanks to Belinda Jones for her masterful copyediting. A special thank-you too to Ciara Farrell, the librarian at the Kennel Club, without whom I probably couldn't have done it. Huge thanks also, in no particular order, to Jon Kean, Janet Menzies, Kevin and Karen Egan, Mary and Jeff Davies, Diana King, Jim Motherwell, Samantha Peters, Michael Waldman, Roger Mugford, Duff Hart-Davis, Nicky Philipps, Malcolm Taylor, Carole Harrisson, Lady Jill Bridges, Meryl Asbury, Will Delamore, Anne Hazelby, Wilson Young, Caroline Kisko, Ian Seath, Zena Thorn-Andrews and Danny Danziger; plus a few others who I cannot name. All of them have been so generous with their time and expertise, proving that people who love dogs are some of the very nicest in the world. And, as always, my lovely agent, Jane Turnbull – another confirmed dog-lover, of course – and my wonderful husband, James, who has taken some convincing, but is infinitely tolerant of my obsession.

Books/Media Consulted

Noble Hounds and Dear Companions by Sophie Gordon, Royal Collections Publications, 2007

Reigning Cats and Dogs by Katherine MacDonogh, Fourth Estate, 1999

Our Princesses and Their Dogs by Michal Chance, John Murray, 1936

The Royal Animals by Michele Brown, WH Allen, 1936

The Corgi by Thelma Gray, Chambers, 1952

Royal Dogs: The Pets of British Sovereigns from Victoria to Elizabeth II by John Montgomery, Fletcher, 1962

Dr Mugford's Casebook: Understanding Dogs and Their Owners, Hutchinson, 1991

Royal Dogs by Macdonald Daly, WH Allen, 1955

Young Elizabeth: The Making of Our Queen by Kate Williams, Weidenfeld & Nicholson, 2012

The Royal Encyclopedia edited by Ronald Allison & Sarah Riddell, Macmillan, 1991

'Queen Elizabeth and Her Corgis: A Love Story' by Michael Joseph Gross, *Vanity Fair*, July 2015

'Bill Meldrum: the Queen's Gundog trainer', *The Shooting Times*, July 2009

'The Queen's Gun Dogs: royal retrievers' by Elizabeth Walton, *The Field*, April 2016

'Faithful Friends: the Queen and her dogs', Paula Lester, *Country Life*, May 2012

Interview with David Nott by Elizabeth Grice, *Daily Telegraph*, January 2015

Interview with David Nott by Kirsty Young, BBC 'Desert Island Discs', June 2016

Picture Acknowledgements